APPALACHIAN MOUNTAIN GIRL

APPALACHIAN MOUNTAIN GIRL

RHODA B. WARREN

ACADEMY CHICAGO PUBLISHERS

Published in 1998 by
Academy Chicago Publishers
363 West Erie Street
Chicago, Illinois 60610

Library of Congress Cataloging-in-Publication Data

Warren, Rhoda B.
    Appalachian Mountain girl / Rhoda B. Warren
      p.   cm.
    ISBN 0-89733-464-7
    1. Warren, Rhoda B. 2. Letcher (Ky.)—Biography. 3.
Mountain life—Kentucky—Letcher Region. 4. Letcher
Region (Ky.)—Social life and customs. 5. Coal miners—
Kentucky—Letcher—Biography.
    I. Title.
F459.L47W37   1998
976.9'163043'092—dc21
[B]   98-26785
                                      CIP

THIS BOOK IS DEDICATED TO MY PARENTS,
LAURA AND FRANK BAILEY

CONTENTS

The author wishes to thank the following individuals: Gilbert Jordan for his encouragement and support, Marsha Leuer, who invested many hours of typing and proofreading the manuscript, and my son Lewis Warren for his valuable assistance.

INTRODUCTION

The scenes in Letcher, Kentucky, after I went away hovered in the backroads of my memory, sometimes consciously, other times subconsciously, but always present at some level. Finally, I seemed compelled to put words to the memories.

From a distance, the sharp, jagged cliffs were softened, the wind blowing over the frozen ground was no longer cold and the once meager table was now more than ample.

Most of the people were now gone, but there, in an unusual gallery, I saw their portraits. They hung on the big trunks of the beech trees along the banks of Crase's Branch in colors so muted and tones so subtle as to be almost invisible except in the clearest light.

At least that was the way it appeared in the outline to write these stories. But, then, the outline wasn't written by pen or paper. No, the outline for these stories flowed in my bloodstream.

Rhoda Warren
November 1998

CORBIN GLOW

Heavy heat hung over the holler from wall to wall on the two mountains that faced each other across a narrow creek and the railroad track. The mountains were so high and steep that there was little more than a cleavage with no valley between them. The trees had been cut, leaving black jagged stumps everywhere.

The hillsides were covered in measured rows of two- and three-room houses made of rough lumber. Only the back walls of the houses rested on the ground. The front walls, to level them with the steepness of the hills, were propped on stilts six to eight feet high. Slimy green bald areas marked places where dishwater had been thrown from kitchen doors. Tin cans rolled as far as the nearest weed patch, where they heaped and caught a glint of the sun even as rust claimed them. A huge pile of blue-black coal lay in each yard, feeding hundreds of cookstoves which filled the air with gritty black smoke.

On one of the mountains was the black gaping maw of a coal mine, its dank cold breathing of the grave. While passersby moved out of its reach, the miners, with lowered heads and stooped shoulders, entered its darkness. A slate dump slid imperceptibly toward the creek in a gray scaly sheath of thin slabs of rock. Smouldering fire and smoke seeped from its edges, a fire no rain would be able to put out.

In this narrow cleft, the heat shimmered over a path of hot black cinders that lay alongside the railroad track; it also shimmered over the creek that floated a film of slow moving coal dust glinting in oily greens and blues. The rocks along the creek bed were a bright orangy-yellow. Their pitted surfaces, penetrated by iron and sulphur, gave them the powdery texture of crepe cloth.

The soundtrack for this nether world was a crashing, earsplitting racket made by tons of coal rolling down the mountain on the grinding gears of a conveyor until it plunged through a chute at a big tipple that straddled the railroad at the bottom. A huge iron railroad car, especially made for coal, sat beneath the chute and caught it from daylight to dark in a roaring crash of rock hitting metal.

Thick clouds of coal dust blown from this blasting inferno picked up an air current and floated off to settle on every leaf of every tree and bush it could reach. The leaves looked as if they had been brushed with gray paint by the hand of Death.

Hundreds of people were wedged in this place. The men were either in the mines or sleeping after the night shift. The women, surrounded by children, sat on porches fanning themselves in slow motion, their minds pondering—pondering only God knew what as they took in their surrealist surroundings.

There were no churches and no cemetery at this new place. The dead were shipped to relatives "back home" from where they'd come, making their last journey on the Louisville & Nashville passenger train.

This was in the dog days of August, 1930 at Corbin Glow, one of the newest and largest mining operations in southeastern Kentucky.

I sat expectantly on the narrow porch of our two-room house, waiting minute by minute for the siren to blow for the changing of the shifts in the mines. In the thick air it had a mournful wail, but its sound was the focal point of my day, all my days, in rain or shine, except in the winter when it would be dark, for the sound meant my father would be coming home. He'd left at dawn before I'd awakened.

At the sound I ran off the porch and halfway up the narrow path that led to the mines. It had been trodden into the color and hardness of concrete by thousands of weary footsteps plodding up and down, to and from the mines. I stepped off it into weeds almost as high as I was and focused my eyes on that black hole in the hillside. The men came out of it half crouching as their heads barely cleared the damp, dripping, timbered roof. In single file they began a slow descent.

They all looked alike. Coal black from head to toe, they wore the same kind of work clothes, the same canvas caps that held a brass carbide lamp fastened to its visor and the same aluminum dinner buckets, in which the bottom half held water. As they slowly filed past, I searched each black face with its white-ringed eyes, trying to identify my father. At last, a figure stepped out of line and took me by the hand. My heart leapt in happiness as I took his empty dinner bucket to carry for him and we walked home with my hand in his.

One night that summer something like a bolt of lightning struck at the supper table. It shattered the house and it changed our lives. Mother began a response to something Father said and in mid-sentence started screaming, "I can't stand another day in this place. I'm not going to live here another day. I'm not going to live here another day."

"Another day. *Another day.*" Father's voice rose louder than hers as he mocked in anger: "You can't stand it another *day.* I have no *day.* I crawl into that goddamned black hole before daylight and half the time I crawl out of that goddamned black hole after dark and you sit here and tell me that you can't stand it another *day.* You don't know what the hell *daylight* means."

I went around the table and stood beside him. The picture he'd just painted of himself alarmed me. I buried my head in his shoulder. Every muscle in his body was tensed into an unrelenting skeleton of steel.

Across the table Mother sat with her head bowed in her hands, weeping.

She was right, we had to leave this ugly place. I went over and stood beside her. She straightened up, wiping the tears and anger from her eyes on the hem of her apron, then went to the stove and in a conciliatory manner gave Father a cup of coffee. In reconciliation he took a sip of it. The storm was over.

"All I meant to say when I got off it was that if we had another place we could have a garden and some chickens and a cow. We could eat better than we do from the company store. That's all I meant to say." She sounded apologetic.

Father stared at her, his face too pale, coal dust still clinging to his eyelashes. He was thinking. He was thinking hard. "Maybe I could find such a place. I'll ask around. We've got enough money right now if I can find the right house." He straightened up in his chair and his shoulders went back a little as the tension slowly lost its grip on his body. Mother had just handed him a key that would unlock the prison.

Father had been raised on a farm, but hated the coaxing of growing things, hated being locked into combat with insects, hated waiting patiently for rain that sometimes didn't come, or sometimes came in such torrents that it washed the crops off the steep hillsides. After his marriage following World War I, he'd given up farming to seek his fortune in the new coal mines.

Now, following the explosive exchange with Mother, he had to wait a few days for the NO WORK TOMORROW sign to appear in the bookkeeper's window at the commissary. He already knew there'd be no work because there were ten cars of coal backed up on the sidetrack. And he already knew there'd be no pay for the lost day.

He put on a clean pair of overalls and a denim shirt, getting ready to go to Letcher to look at a place one of the miners had told him about. I went to the door and asked if I could go with him.

Mother said, "No, you can't walk six miles there and back."

"Yes I can." I kept walking across the porch.

"Maybe she can," Father said, somewhat doubtfully.

For about two miles, we walked down the railroad track's elongated curves that made the road seem almost straight as it followed the creek out of the holler. Suddenly, with barely a sign of terrain change, we walked into a place so narrow that the light in it was dim. One of the mountains was pushing the railroad against the creek. The one on the other side, rising from a solid granite base, was blocking any further movement, leaving us in a narrow crevice of steel and rock.

My heart thumped, terrified that a train would come roaring through and where could we go? Father walked ahead and seldom looked back. He knew that the trains never stopped blowing on curves, but I didn't. Adding to my fear, I couldn't walk and breathe and talk at the same time on these broad ties since they were about two inches farther apart than my normal stride. I had to give a little hop and leap, first on one foot, then the other, to reach them and the exertion made it impossible to ask anything. Finally, I could hardly take another step.

As suddenly as we'd walked into this place, we stepped out of it through a narrow exit into sunlight again. I stopped in amazement. In front of my eyes a broad river was flowing serenely past this dark chasm. Low foothills on the far side had clumps of green bushes everywhere and there before me grew all the crayon flowers that I'd ever painted. They had somehow escaped the rough flat paper that I'd drawn them on and planted themselves firmly in this new and wonderful landscape.

When I turned back to the railroad, it had all but disappeared and Father with it. I could see a stretch of rail about a mile away as the track came out of a deep curve. Forcing my legs on I walked into the deep mile-long curve.

Out of reach of the river's flooding, the railroad track here was raised about ten feet. It had been dynamited out of solid rock into a curving wall a mile long and three stories high. Big trees at its top gave the cliff the appearance of ending in the sky. Its minute ledges held tufts of grass. Its crowbarred grooves were full of dead leaves and here and there a scraggly bush grew straight outward. Threading through all this were narrow, erratic seams of coal. From where I stood the hot steel rails flowed against the rock wall like molten silver.

"I need a drink of water," I called to Father, my throat so dry it could barely make a sound. "Right out here," he pointed toward the middle of the cliff without looking back. I hopped and leaped on till he finally stopped and waited for me to catch up. The water ran down a moss-covered groove in the cliff, met a little basin, stopped to overflow into a pile of mouldy leaves from last winter and disappeared under the cliff. Opening my mouth, I scooped up palmsful of cold water tasting pleasantly of tree roots and old leaves. I went back to the railroad and sat down on the end of a tie beside Father. "Are you tired?" he asked.

I didn't dare say yes. "No, I'm not tired, but my knees hurt from all this hopping and my feet hurt too." I was humiliated to hear a whimpering sound in my voice.

"Hopping? Why are you hopping?"

I explained why.

"Why don't you walk on the path?" He pointed along the river bank. From there on to where we turned off, I walked on the soft earthy path. It soothed my feet and I could hear the river moving over the big rocks in a low grinding murmur.

At last we came to a rough dirt road that turned up a small creek toward a little store. It sat perched so securely on an outcrop of rock that the wide ledges in the rock's facing were used as steps to it. Big beech trees lined the creek that flowed not ten feet away.

Inside was cool and shady. I sat in one of the big rockers, each with a thick hickory splint bottom, which circled a cold iron stove full of rusty spots. A dog, from habit, lay close to the stove. Without lifting his head, he opened both eyes wide, looked into each face and went back to sleep.

Lige Banks, the storekeeper, took Father to look at a property owned by Buck Tramer and priced at $200. Father agreed on the spot to buy the house. I stayed behind with Mrs. Banks.

Returning, Father took a Prince Albert tobacco can from his pocket, opened it up and carefully counted out $200 into the hand of Mr. Banks. Then he selected two little cans of Vienna sausages, each with a tiny key fastened to its side to open it, a box of crackers and two Coco-Colas for our lunch. He handed Mr. Banks a handful of coins.

"I don't take Corbin Glow scrip, Mr. Bailey. The company won't redeem it and I can't walk that far to trade it out."

Father was embarrassed. He'd brought only two hundred dollars in cash to pay for the house.

"I'll put it on time. You'll be coming back." Mr. Banks smiled.

Even though it was August, we ate lunch sitting around the stove. Mr. Banks made himself a thick baloney sandwich smeared with mustard, helped himself to a cold Orange Crush and joined us at the stove. He had a strange look that I hadn't seen before. He was pudgy, even his hands were pudgy. His face had a pink glow unlike any man's face I'd ever seen and there wasn't a mote of coal dust about his being.

He and Father talked of these new coal mines which were being dug in the mountainsides all over southeastern Kentucky, bringing people from farms and towns to get rich quick with this "black gold"; of how big Eastern interests were buying all the timberlands from people who could hardly read or write.

"Yes, Mr. Bailey, you're doin' the right thing coming here, gettin' on solid ground. Mining camps are hard places to live in," said Mr. Banks.

As they talked on and on, I compared his little store with its 25-pound bags of stone-ground corn meal, its big jugs of molasses and its whole peaches, canned with the pits and studded with cloves, to the company commissary's chrome-and-white enamel coolers full of meal, ice cream and pop; its big butcher's block that seemed to cut nothing but pork chops; its shelves full of cornflakes with nothing but Pet Milk to go with them; its long rows of flimsy "light bread" that, Mother said, "a dog wouldn't eat." Father would tell her, "But we black-faced bastards have to eat that or nothing."

People who'd been to Whitesburg said food cost twice as much in Corbin Glow. A bitter hatred was slowly building against the mining companies and in a very few years it would explode in dynamite and gunfire.

Father shook hands with Mr. Banks and his wife and we left, walking home more slowly. The sun had set behind the mountain of the big hot curve and in its cooler shadow we rested a time or two. My thoughts were happily on the little store and the beautiful, willowy Nancy Banks with her friendly blue eyes. She'd given me a bar of candy as we left and asked me, as she held my hand, to come back.

An icy dread suddenly overwhelmed me. We'd come to the portals of that dark crevice which was the doorway to Corbin Glow mines. I stopped, took a deep breath and walked through it without incident.

Mother had supper waiting and we gathered around the table.

"I don't want a question asked till I've finished supper." Father looked into each pair of eyes and each pair of eyes dropped to the plate. "And that means everybody," he added.

The one-course supper was over in ten minutes flat because we couldn't wait to hear all the details of our new home. Like a convict having been released after years of incarceration, Father described the world he'd just found. "It's the prettiest place on earth. You can see far off; a big level place with gardens right down in bottom lands. You'll see a storm comin' long 'fore it strikes." He turned to Mother, "They ain't a mine in sight and the leaves on the trees are as green as green can be. And they're full of birds."

"What are birds?" one of my young brothers asked.

"What are birds?" Father asked, astonished. "You've all seen pictures of birds. Now, in the next few days help your mother get packed. We're movin' Sunday." He waved us from the table.

Sunday morning the big company coal truck came early. The iron cookstove and the iron bedsteads were put in it and then everything else was thrown on top and roped down. We had barely enough belongings to fill the truck.

Mother, holding a baby, rode with Father and the driver. The rest of us, sitting in back on an old quilt, held onto the tailgate. Like refugees from a John Steinbeck novel, we set forth to "the prettiest place on earth": Letcher, Kentucky.

ARRIVING IN LETCHER

The truck which had shivered, shaken and lurched its way from the Corbin Glow mining camp over stony, dirt roads full of holes, finally came to a stop at a front gate. Nobody moved. We sat staring at the house.

The house was on a hillside so that when Mother leaned over to look through the window on the driver's side of the truck, she had to look upward to see it. She truly saw "a mansion." It was the first real home she had ever had. I could hardly believe what I saw myself. Approached through a narrow lane, fenced in on both sides, the house had been all but hidden by a clump of trees.

Now sedately standing there was our house! It had two rooms sixteen-by-sixteen feet each with a glass-paneled door, and a window opening onto an eight-foot-wide front porch with a railing around it. Each room had a little fireplace with a concrete hearth and a small iron grate to burn coal. The mantel in one room was made of oak and had a mirror in it. This room would eventually be the sitting room, even with beds and chairs in it, and be called "the middle room." Of course we didn't see all this from the truck.

Four stone steps led up to the gate, with a peach tree on either side of it. Across the yard nine rough wide board steps led up to the front porch. Six four-by-four posts held up the front of the house. The back of the house rested on rocks embedded in the hillside.

In a corner of the yard was an ash tree. A little creek came down the hill about ten feet from the room in which I would sleep. The creek went from the summer silence of a dry creek bed, interspersed with an occasional storm which overflowed it across the yard, under the porch and out through the front gate, to a frozen sheet in January.

Father ordered the truck driver to go around the house to the back. "It'll be easier to set the stove to the kitchen," he said. Since Father's days in the army as a sergeant, he no longer made polite requests, if he ever had.

Mother was tugging at my shoulder. "We've got to unload the truck. We can't stand here all day." She shoved the baby in my arms and walked away.

It was then that I saw the building in the back yard about twenty feet up the hill from the main house. Mother said that it was the kitchen and explained how cool the "big house" would be in the summer without a coal stove heating it. "I can hang the wash on that porch on rainy Mondays." She went on and on about how lucky she was to have the kitchen away from the house.

The "kitchen" was about sixteen-by-sixteen feet square, made of unpainted pine lumber with a peaked roof from which a chimney protruded. Its front was about six feet off the ground and sat on wooden posts because of the steepness of the hill. The door was at the back corner of the kitchen building which rested on the ground, so we didn't have to climb steep stairs.

When the truck backed across the creek to get nearer the gate, I could see why Father found it easier to get the big iron stove in through the entrance. They still had to carry the heavy thing up the hill.

The "big house" was left empty, save for two metal beds, an iron baby crib and an old trunk. The children ran and played in it while Mother and the baby stayed daytimes in the kitchen house. As the year passed, the main house would have curtains and be filled with beds and chairs. But for now . . .

There was a well near the back of the main house about halfway between the house and the kitchen. It was deep and lined with rocks. A square wooden box was built around its top and a metal bucket hung from a rope on a pulley. The water in it was icy cold. The well was one of Mother's major worries, because the children liked to climb up on it and look down. For this infraction she "set their bottoms afire" with her hand.

A little smokehouse in the backyard was barely out of reach of the creek. "Up the holler aways" was an outhouse. Mother had a latch put way up high on it so the little ones couldn't get in. In the backyard, which became our playground, we had to lean our heads back to see the top of the mountain.

After the stove with its big, black metal pipes had been installed, Mother settled the kitchen with the white enamel-topped table, a few chairs and a kitchen cabinet which held the skillets, kettles and a few dishes. The kitchen cabinet had a flour bin with a built-in sifter.

With the three of them working, the house was settled in about an hour and the truck was gone, severing us completely from Corbin Glow.

As we had no coal yet, Father gathered wood from the hillside and built a fire. Mother baked a pan of cornbread and fried a skillet of potatoes for supper.

The sun set early behind the mountain; long shade over the house slowly deepened into a cool twilight. The children, in a strange place, huddled close to Mother as the whippoorwills began their strange cry.

A long hello came from our front gate and Mother sent me down the path and around the house to answer it. An old woman stood there with a large water bucket in her hand. "Go git yo' daddy, honey," she requested. I ran around the house and up the path to get Father. He looked surprised as we approached the gate. "Mister Bailey," she said, "Mister Banks told me about you." Father opened the gate. "Step in."

She stepped in, and as Father closed the gate, she said, "Mr. Tramel lets me draw drinkin' water here. I don't have a well. I have a creek for wash water."

"Come out to the back. You're welcome to the water."

She followed him to the back yard and drew a bucket of water. Mother, with a baby on her hip, joined them and the stranger introduced herself. Her name was Miss Kelly. ("Miss" was used in Letcher for "Mrs." The married women hadn't figured out how to wrap their tongues around an "R" in the middle of an "M" and an "S." Some of the aged men and women still used the old word "Mistress").

Miss Kelly said she was a widow with eight children. Her husband had been killed in the mine in a slate fall. She had a cow and a big garden, but alas, no well. She was a large woman with wide hips. Her breasts, underneath a thin cotton dress, sagged nearly to her belt line. Her hair was dark, almost black, even though she was elderly. It was worn in a wispy knot at the back of her head and topped with a frayed straw hat. She wore a pair of men's old floppy slippers, explaining that she had "bad feet."

Miss Kelly had a warm smile and an appealing personality. Her trips to draw water soon became the highlights of Mother's days. She dropped everything for the visit. Later, if we were eating supper when Miss Kelly came, Mother would get her a chair and put another plate on the table over Miss Kelly's protests that she had just eaten. Sitting down, she'd say, "I'll just take a bite" while she filled her plate.

In the mornings, as she and Mother talked at the well, I began to admire Miss Kelly no end. She knew what everybody in Letcher was doing or thinking of doing. As Mother didn't know anybody yet, she didn't add much but an occasional, "Lord in Heaven, is that the truth?" to some shocking revelation. "That's the truth if I *ever* told it," Miss Kelly would reply. Miss Kelly's "shocking revelations" were mostly about unusual births or deaths or a new daughter-in-law who wasn't adjusting to her in-laws' home.

With the woods around us full of wild grapevines to swing on, my brothers and I ran around in the heat of the day climbing mountains and trees and wading creeks. By the end of the week, we were so punctured, scratched, stung and sunburned that Mother confined us to the yard for awhile.

After my skinned knees healed, I found a more gentle pursuit. I learned to make dresses. I pinned huge paw-paw leaves together with hawthorns, leaving a hole for my head and adding sleeves. These dresses were so fragile that by nightfall they would be shrunken and dried up.

The most memorable dress I made had a long train. I pinned buttercups around the neckline with the thorns and tied the tough stems of daisies together for a belt. I carried the fragile garment through the underbrush and waited till I reached our back gate to put it on. Then, with my head high, I swept through the back yard like a queen. I expected my mother to say, "What a beautiful dress!" Instead, she said "Where in God's name have you been so long? This house don't run by itself. Now git that thing off and git busy." I wilted faster than my dress did.

Mother's enthusiasm for the outside kitchen died a slow, lingering death, beginning a few weeks after we moved in and lasting till the middle of January. One morning it began to rain and poured for two days. We all got soaking wet going to and fro for our meals. The steep path to the kitchen got so muddy and slippery, we often slid down. We'd eat in our damp clothes and then get wetter going back to the main house.

As winter came on, the evening dew on the path would be frozen into an icy glaze by daylight. As we ran up the path our bare feet burned and became almost blistered. When we got there, the kitchen would be warm and Mother would have a hot breakfast ready but her face was set in an ugly frown.

One evening she announced to Father, "I'm going to start cooking in the big house on one of these fireplaces!

I can't put these children through this any longer and I'm sick of it myself!" Father didn't say a word for the longest time, and then, "Well, I'll have the kitchen moved down here!" Mother was speechless.

A huge square space the size of the kitchen was dug out of the side of the mountain at the back of one of the rooms of the main house. The well box was removed and the well covered with boards. Then the kitchen with its chimney and porch removed was lowered on logs with the help of three men and, by a lot of maneuvering, was finally placed against a wall of the house.

A doorway was cut from the kitchen into the next room. Later Father built a wide L-shaped porch at the back of the house and added two long wooden benches. Mother added a swing and two rockers to the front porch and our house was complete. At last!

GOING TO SCHOOL

L etcher was in Letcher County in the mountainous section of southeastern Kentucky. It wasn't a village, nor, in a sense, was it a community. The wide, deep Rockhouse Creek, referred to as "The River," and the L&N Railroad following it curve by curve, cut the settlement in two.

While the people on both sides of the river did intermingle, there were definitely two groups of neighbors. The men on our side of the river were mostly miners. There were two rows of camp houses plus a colored camp left over from a worked-out mine. On the other side of Rockhouse Creek the men were mostly farmers. They had a slaughterhouse, a grist mill and a lumberyard. Our side had the post office and two little stores and it was here across a wooden bridge that people from both sides usually met.

About a mile from Letcher, Rockhouse Creek emptied into the north fork of the Kentucky River at Blackey, a village which lay between Whitesburg and Hazard. Blackey had a train station, a movingpicture house, many stores and two or three churches.

The day we arrived in Letcher, I scrambled over the tailgate and was helping my brothers down when the young truck driver saw me staring at the cluster of brick buildings in the distance surrounded by a high wire fence. "That's Stuart Robinson School," he told me.

I was nearly eight years old and I'd been to school exactly one day. At six years old I started school in Corbin Glow where I sat on a bench in a row of children next to a boy, who, like all boys there in summer, had shaved his head. His hair had grown back in thistle-like spikes. His sunburned face was fiery red and he kept wiping his muddy shoes on my white stockings. "I'm not going to school again," I told Mother when I got home that day. "I had to sit by a burr-head who rubbed mud on my stockings!"

"Well, if that's the way school is, you don't have to go back."

I hadn't been back yet, for neither Father nor Mother had gone to discuss this incident with the teacher.

In the meantime, I had learned to read somewhat. Father read the *Louisville Courier Journal* which the L&N train dropped off in a bundle at the Corbin Glow commissary. I'd put my finger under a big black caption and Father would read aloud something like: "Woman Drowns" or "Man Shot" and I'd read it back to him. I quickly learned those words because they were in the paper every day. I also learned a lot of smaller words.

Mother tried to help me learn to read. She started with "The Little Red Hen," but stumbled so badly over words with more than three letters that I dreaded listening to her.

As I stood staring at those buildings in the distance, I couldn't believe that a school could be that big. Then and there I decided to go back to school. I started that September. By that time, I'd made the acquaintance of the children in the neighborhood. The first morning, when they came down the paths and through the lanes that converged on the main road, I joined them to walk to school. The school was surrounded by a high chain-link fence. To get over it we had to climb a stile. On the outside we went up a slanted ladder made of three-inch metal pipes. There was a landing on top. We went down ordinary steps on the inside.

I was eight years old and in the first grade with children six years old. Miss Mary Ervin, a tall, dignified woman from Georgia, taught first, second and third grades in one big room. The first grade lessons consisted of nothing more than getting the alphabet settled in one's brain and then learning how to pronounce the letter and its variants and how to print and write it. We started each class repeating phonetically in unison with Miss Ervin: "A" (as in take), a (as in cat) and a (as in Father), while she kept her pointer on the "A." She told us that an "A" had to tell its name if the word ended in "E" (as in made and tale). I couldn't wait each day to get to school to say all those letters. As we learned them by repetition, we began to render them in a sing-song tone.

Two months later, with her hand on my shoulder, Miss Ervin said "You may move into the second grade." She helped me move my papers and my one book across the aisle into the next class. Here we learned to read with our finger moving from word to word while she read a story to us. She read slowly and in a few days we were each, in turn, asked to get up and read the story to the class. I loved words, but in arithmetic I had to memorize the figures and count on my fingers to make it come out right and sometimes it didn't.

Two months after that, Miss Ervin leaned over my desk and said, "You may move into the third grade." It was here that I ran into trouble with Miss Ervin, for this was the grade in which we learned to spell. Every Friday the third grade stood up, backs to the blackboard, and Miss Ervin went down the front line calling out words from that week's lessons. When a student missed a word, he had to sit down. There were only two or three pupils left standing when the lesson ended. But now . . . "Next," from Miss Ervin meant my turn. Looking directly at me, "Awgon," she intoned.

"Awgon?" I panicked. Had I studied the wrong lesson?

"Awgon" she repeated. I stared at her in silence.

"Next," she said, moving to the next person as I took my seat. I went up to her desk later and told her that I had looked up all the words in the spelling lessons and that "Awgon" wasn't in *my* book. She picked up the speller, "It's right here, my dear." She thrust it under my eyes with her finger beside the word "organ."

Many of the teachers were from the deep south and our mountain dialect clashed, not only with pronunciation, but in word meanings.

When I told Mother about this spelling incident, she told Father that with all these foreign teachers, "our children ain't never goin' to learn to talk right."

Many of Stuart Robinson's teachers were from wealthy, cultured homes with proper manners and high morals. Their backgrounds were unimpeachable. They worked there for their church missions for little or no money.

Miss McNeil, the music teacher, was short and plump. Even with her hair coiled high on her head, she was still short. But Napoleon never had the command of his troops which Miss McNeil had over hers. At 11:30 sharp each day, with one of the high school music students playing the piano, we marched into chapel two-by-two in perfect step to the music and in strict military precision. We marched up the aisle to the front and then the students split, those on the right filing into the right-hand seats and those in the left into the opposite seats. Miss McNeil stood at the podium, her sharp blue eyes searching for a flagging step, her baton vigorously beating time to "Onward Christian Soldiers." That was the marching song of the Stuart Robinson School. We were all there, from first grade to senior high, 150 strong, marching to war against ungodliness.

Miss Virginia Byrd, the school nurse, was from Virginia and connected with one of that state's great families. A local mother had named her beautiful daughter Virginia Byrd Asher. She was in my class and she was always called, clearly and distinctly, Virginia-Byrd. Miss Byrd examined the students weekly, class by class, one by one, for head lice, dirty fingernails, enlarged tonsils, etc. She had my mouth open one day when she asked, "Don't you ever brush your teeth?"

"No."

"Why not?"

"I don't know."

"You don't have a toothbrush?"

I shook my head, no. I'd never even seen a toothbrush.

She smiled, "Well, we'll fix that." Reaching into a little box from her black "doctor's bag," she handed me a four-inch long twig from a birch tree. "You just chew the end of it to break the fibers into a little broom-like thing." I chewed and swallowed the sweet birch juice. Taking the twig from my hand she said, "You see, now you have a toothbrush. Dampen it in water and dip it into baking soda and brush your teeth every day."

It was in Letcher in the 1920s that the Southern Presbyterian Church had established a model boarding school called the Stuart Robinson School.

Blackey had been chosen originally for the school site, but when the plans were drawn for the buildings, football field and gardens, there wasn't enough level ground for it in Blackey, so the church purchased sixteen acres of rolling land in Letcher. There was room for a modern dairy barn, cornfields and acres of vegetables.

The founding of the Stuart Robinson School was the direct result of groundwork laid by Rev. E. O. Guerrant, who, as a young lieutenant serving in Morgan's army during the Civil War, had been through the southern Appalachian region and had seen the need for schools there.

Dr. Guerrant in his book, *Galax Gatherers*, described his trip through a narrow valley at the headwaters of the Kentucky River twenty-five miles from the Virginia border:

> The trail led us down Black Mountain, as nearly perpendicular as a man could walk or a mule could ride.

At the foot we struck the Poor Fork of the Cumberland River. (These people have a genius for giving
appropriate names). A few miles down one fork and
up another brought us to the Cumberland Mountain . . .
It ought to be called Stone Mountain, for it is a mass
of stones from top to bottom . . . and hard to climb on
account of the multitude of stones which fill the narrow gully that is called a road. I once rode a mule to
the top of Pike's Peak and I don't know which is the
worse road.

He arrived at the foot of Pine Mountain on the
Whitesburg side with every bone aching, and wrote, "I
am glad I am alive."

Dr. Guerrant was a practicing physician at the time
he made this army trek but after the war he decided to
devote his life to helping the Appalachian people. He at-
tended Union Theological Seminary in Virginia and came
back to the area to preach, determined to put Presbyterian
churches and schools in those mountains.

He described the people in this region as pure Anglo-
Saxon: "They were a people intelligent; a people ambi-
tious; . . . but a people who, because of two hundred years
of isolation, had become very individualistic. Hardships
of every kind, disease, ignorance and extreme poverty
were companions in many homes."

Coming back as a minister, he told of preaching to
Kentuckians in a little court house at Whitesburg. Later
he said of them:

These hardy mountaineers are among the finest specimens of manhood, with strong minds and bodies and

only need conversion to make them fine specimens of Christian activity. Long training in extreme views of God's sovereignty and man's inability has made them the hardest people to reach I have ever known. It is humanly impossible to reach the man with a hard heart and a hard head."

And so, many years later, the Southern Presbyterian Church was carrying out Dr. Guerrant's dream and operating this model school for about 150 boys and girls from the Appalachians who boarded there. The students worked their way to graduation. The boys were up before daybreak to milk the cows and clean the barn. They painted the buildings and mowed the lawns. They worked the fields and gardens, learning modern farming methods which included operating and repairing tractors and mowers.

The girls did the laundry, cleaned windows and floors and, under a qualified cook, cooked the meals and canned hundreds of jars of fruit and vegetables, jams and jellies.

Local children who didn't live in the dormitories were allowed to attend the school free as day students. Some of them walked to school four or five miles each way.

When Mr. Guerrant wrote that the people here "only need conversion and culture to make them fine specimens of Christian activity," he could not have foreseen that the "culture" the students would receive would, for a while, create a schism between some of the students and their parents. The young left the old churches—the "hard-shell" Baptists and the high-powered, popular "Holy Rollers." The boys at the school learned enough carpentry so they would not patch up outbuildings with old pieces of tin, or prop up the front porch with a pile of rocks. All some of their fathers ever said was, "Hit warn't necessary."

The girls began to cook things besides pinto beans and cornbread. They stopped stringing green beans with a needle and heavy thread, like beads, to hang from a nail on the porch to dry (Leather Britches). They made no more "sulferated" apples. They now drank their milk straight without churning it for buttermilk. Some of the mothers were aghast when their kitchens were invaded by their "educated" daughters.

Soon after I became a student at the Stuart Robinson School, I brought Mother an invitation to a Mother and Daughter church supper at Blackey. We went. The food was different from anything we'd ever eaten before. Roasted chicken? She'd always fried chicken or cooked it with dumplings. Mashed potatoes? She'd always fried potatoes or boiled them with their skins on. Asparagus she knew as "Spar Grass." Its feathery foliage was used only in the back of flower beds. Yeasty rolls? She had never tasted one. She made biscuits every morning and cornbread for every dinner. Jello—with cherries? We'd never seen anything remotely like it. The big three-layered Martha Washington cakes? No! Mother always made two-layered gingerbread cakes put together with dried apples.

We did try to make the Jello thing at home, but we didn't know that you made it only in winter if you didn't have a refrigerator. We watched it for several days waiting for it to gel.

Mother lived to be seventy-five years old, but she never changed her way of cooking.

ITHAL

One evening Miss Kelly's daughter, Ithal (Eye-thal), came with her to get water. She was a few years older than I, petite, with dark hair and eyes. I'd never met anybody with whom I was so entranced. "Different" was not the word. She was out of my world totally. Her hair, cut by herself in a simulated "shingle bob," and a little dab of rouge on her cheekbones gave her face the look of a beautiful china doll. Her fingernails were bright red, her dress almost showed her knees and she wore spike heel shoes. I stared at Ithal all evening. Yes, I wanted to look exactly like her, except for her rough red hands, which seemed out of place with the rest of her.

After they had drawn their water and left, I looked at Mother expectantly—knowing she must have compared Ithal to her stringy-haired freckle-faced daughter who wore slouchy dresses and went barefoot. "Pore Miss Kelly," Mother said mournfully, "Havin' a daughter like that, that does nothin' in this world but primp." I was happy that Mother liked me, but I was unhappy that she didn't like Ithal.

Miss Kelly's children were grown up and all had left home except a son and Ithal.

I was the same height as Ithal and over time we became friends. She lived close by, and I stopped at her house often.

Ithal did laundry for the boys in Stuart Robinson's dormitory, washing and ironing a large canvas bag full for fifty cents. She heated the creek water on the stove and scrubbed the clothes clean on a washboard with Fels Naptha soap. This scrubbing is what made her hands so red and rough, but it gave her more money to spend on herself than most women in Letcher had. She confided one day that she hoped to get a husband "with means" and that a man "with means" wanted a woman who knew how to live "with means."

As I grew older, my friendship with Ithal deepened. Forbidden fruit is irresistible. Sitting on her front porch, she gave me a picture of life as it really was. No one knew this better than Ithal, for she avidly read *True Confessions* magazine. One day she lent me one of these and I hurried home with it. Sitting by the little coal fire, I began reading the heartbreaking story of "The Sharecropper's Daughter." The rich owner's son had made her pregnant. It was winter, cold and frosty, when her cruel father ordered her out of the house. I raised my knuckle to wipe away a tear when a big hand lifted the magazine from my lap. It was my father. He tore it in two and laid it on the fire.

"Can't you find somethin' better to read?"

I didn't answer, but I doubted it.

Mother had followed him into the room. "She gets all this foolishness from Ithal."

"If you wouldn't let her run around from house to house she wouldn't be bringin' this trash home!"

"Well, I'll try to keep her home more," Mother feebly promised. While they were carrying on, I'd laid plans to read the rest of the story.

The next day when Mother sent me to Blackey to get a gallon of kerosene for the lamps, I went to Mr. Boggs' grocery store, where newspapers and magazines were sold. I looked aimlessly at one shelf after another till he got busy waiting on a customer. Then I picked up *True Confessions* and quickly read the last two pages.

The screw-on lid for the long spout of the metal kerosene can had been lost. The spout was closed with a raw potato pushed down over it. As I walked home across the high train trestle which crossed the Kentucky River, I could smell kerosene which had jostled out around the potato. I paid little attention. My mind was on the sharecropper's daughter who had died an untimely death in childbirth.

One day Miss Kelly came to tell Mother that she had been called to her son's home in Nashville because of illness in the house and that she'd be gone for a few days. She asked Mother if I could stay nights with Ithal. "She'll need a little comp'ny."

Early that evening, after a dozen "do's and don'ts" from Mother which went in one ear and out the other, I went to Ithal's house. I was shocked the minute I walked in. She was wearing red silk pajamas tied at the waist with a fringed silk sash! She laughed at the surprised look on my face. "Everbidy in the city wears these." Then noticing the old faded nightgown rolled up under my arm, she added, "Well, not everybidy, flannel gowns are warmer." I didn't envy her. The long flannel gown I carried felt like security when I compared it to what would befall me if I pranced around in our house in red silk britches. After another lecture from Ithal on how to get a man "with means," we each settled down with *True Confessions* and didn't say another word till we said "Goodnight" and went to bed. This was one tale I wouldn't go home and tell Mother, for she had already begun referring to Ithal as "Jezebel."

Next morning, after shedding the silk pajamas, Ithal built a fire in the stove. Then with brown sugar and water, she boiled a smooth rich syrup to go with buckwheat pancakes which she served with fresh-made butter, white and light and with a hint of sour cream about it. She poured me a cup of coffee and, in imitation of her, I elegantly sipped the bitter brew for the first time. After breakfast she went back to the stove and cooked a bowl of oatmeal which she sprinkled with brown sugar and covered with milk. Picking up a small pan with water in it and taking a towel, she left the room through a door which opened from the back of the kitchen. Returning immediately, she picked up the bowl of oatmeal and, motioning me to follow, said "Come see Eleanor," which she pronounced "Ella Nore."

We started toward a large white iron baby crib with both sides up like a cage. Halfway across the room I stopped in horror. The person in the crib was almost as long as the bed. A more deformed creature was unimaginable. Twisted arms and legs were constantly, almost imperceptibly, writhing. Ithal leaned over the crib. "Eleanor, this is my friend I told you about."

I walked closer to the crib and saw her thick auburn hair styled in pin-curl fashion. "Eleanor is twelve years old, aren't you, Eleanor?" Not a sound came from Eleanor. Her dark fringed eyes were as vacant as an empty house. It was then that I noticed her bright pink nail polish. Ithal let down the side of the crib and fed her the oatmeal which kept trickling down her chin. She told Eleanor where their mother had gone and when she would be back.

"You like to sit on Mother's lap, don't you, Eleanor?"

Silence. Ithal chatted on till the oatmeal was gone. Then, wetting the corner of a towel, she washed Eleanor's face, removed the wet diaper, washed her some more and put on a dry diaper. She leaned over, kissed Eleanor's cheek, pulled up the crib side and we left the room.

Mother was dumbfounded when I told her about Eleanor, the daughter whom Miss Kelly had never mentioned. It was two years later when Mother finally saw Eleanor. She was then in her coffin in the Kelly's middle room with the fireplace lit. It was winter and there were no flowers. Eleanor was wearing a handmade gathered white cotton shroud with lace around the neckline. It covered her distorted body. The only things noticeable were her beautiful hair and the pink painted nails. Mother had long since stopped calling Ithal a Jezebel.

Miss Rainey

Miss Rainey was a widow with only one son. Her husband, Tom, had been assigned to the same measured "room" in the mines as my father, limiting them to the precise area in which they were allowed to dig and load coal. A huge slab of slate had fallen on Tom one day a few feet from where Father was shoveling. Father raised the slate with a jack and, pushing a large block of coal under it, went for help, but Tom was dead. At his funeral there was no coal dust on his face, nor was there the pallor of death. Tom's face was black and blue from being crushed by the slate.

His widow was tall and thin with a high open forehead and a pile of silvery hair punctured here and there with big brown celluloid hairpins. Her blue eyes were always right to the point, with no shifty meanderings as she talked. As mistress of her estate, she carried her affairs on shoulders that hardships couldn't stoop. People admired her skill in taking off a rattlesnake's head at an unbelievable distance with her long black rifle. Her son had gone away and seldom came back. His picture, in which he wore a cap and gown from some far-away school, sat on the mantelpiece.

Because of a rolling slope in the mountain, Miss Rainey's house huddled out of sight of the world that she was so curious about. Just the roof could be seen by the nearest neighbors. The house sat at the foot of a hill with only the creek between it and the beginning rise of another mountain. Small and painted a deep bottle-green, it all but disappeared in the two big porches wrapped around it.

Crase's Branch flowed through its rocky confinement within fifteen feet of Miss Rainey's porch. Here the creek's walls disappeared and the water dropped about three feet, spreading out over a huge, flat rock ledge that went under the supports of the porch, although the water didn't come quite that far. In summer the water flowed so shallow that it barely glazed the bedrock. Trees on both sides of the creek came together overhead, roofing it in shaded greens. The reflections of the green house and the green leaves were so intense that the water was almost black.

On the other side of the house, by the lane, the yard overflowed with flowers. Vines crept up, over and across and then grew away from the fence, well-box and porch railings which bore morning glories, honeysuckle and rambling roses. A row of green glass canning jars, turned upside down, covered rose cuttings—filtering the sun and holding moisture till the slips took and grew tiny plants. The porch was lined with discarded pots and rusty tin cans with blooms of such variations and scents that it took my breath. As I admired them, they said "Miss Rainey is a very beautiful woman." She'd give me beautiful bouquets to take home to Mother, who would look at them longingly and say, "With our yard full of children, flowers here would all get tromped down."

A neighbor had taken Miss Rainey to court the year before in a boundary dispute concerning a few feet of property that lay near the creek. After the court settled in Miss Rainey's favor, she closed off her lane that the neighbor's sons used to get to school, or to haul their coal through. The lane lay between two parallel wire fences, one outlining a cornfield, the other fencing Miss Rainey's house and gardens. The lane was about six feet wide with a slight rise in it toward one end. At the gate to her back yard where a feed box was nailed halfway up on a fencepost, Miss Rainey milked her cow. The lane was filled with cow splatterings that she was constantly shoveling up for her gardens.

The lane had always been open to the people to use as a shortcut to get to the post office and store down by the pike. But after the dispute, Miss Rainey had made a six-foot-wide gate out of fence wire and planks to close one entrance, and for the other one she had a pile of posts and tree branches about five feet high with a few old boards nailed together here and there to block the roadway.

The people now crossed the creek and climbed the point of the ridge to take another road leading from the holler, leaving Miss Rainey in isolation. Being forced to walk an extra mile didn't dispose them to stop and chat when they met her on the pike. They merely nodded and kept walking. But Father always lifted his hat to Miss Rainey and stopped to comment on this and that for a few minutes. He hadn't forgotten Tom Rainey lying under that slab of slate.

One day I came out of school about fifteen minutes after the closing bell had rung. There'd be no bus waiting for me so I could have stayed half an hour longer. The teacher always had time for the students. I had gone up to her desk after the bell and, extending my finger, told her that I had taken a piece of hide off it. After examining it, she cleansed the grubby finger with alcohol and wrapped it in a sterile bandage. Then, taking my hand in hers, she said, "Animals have hides, hides that make shoes and belts. People have skin. Will you remember that?" I never forgot it.

After standing on the steps of the large brick building for a minute, I went down the hill on the cement walk, then climbed the stile that went over the fence enclosing the campus. In Letcher, cows, pigs, chickens and dogs roamed the world at will. The people kept themselves fenced in.

The students were out of sight when I got on the road to home. It was late November following an unusually warm Indian summer. I was surprised to see how much colder it had gotten since morning. Now an icy wind spitting hard granules of snow began to freeze me. I had no stockings and in no time my legs were turning blue and my hair was damp with snow.

At the creek I made an impulsive decision to go through Miss Rainey's lane. I could cut off a mile and be home in fifteen minutes. I told myself I'd walk through it so fast she'd never see me. I climbed over the debris placed at that end. The logs, posts and planks felt stone cold and were damp with freezing snow. Inside, I took a few cautious steps, slowed by my conscience, then defiantly walked on. Suddenly lunging toward me from over the rise was Miss Rainey's huge red Guernsey cow followed by Miss Rainey herself, whacking its flanks with a long stick. Trying to avoid the stick, the cow plunged from side to side of the narrow lane, making the big brass bell around her thick neck clang wildly. There was no place for me to go to get out of her way. I leaned back into the fence so hard that my body made a dent in the wire.

Suddenly, the cow was no longer between me and Miss Rainey's stick. She stopped in surprise, staring at me huddled in the fence. Not only was I shivering with cold, I was now shaking in fear. I had no excuse on earth for trespassing on her property. Pulling myself out of the fence and looking into her eyes, I said, "It's a very cold day."

"Yes, hit is." Her voice showed no feeling. The cow had meandered on down the lane and turned into an opening in the fence toward the cow shed.

"Miss Kelly's cow didn't come home last night at milk time. They're looking for her today. She don't have a cow shed." I blurted on and on. Miss Rainey's stony face relaxed, questioning curiosity filling her eyes, while at the same time she noticed my shivering.

"Why don't you come in the house and get warm and tell Polly 'bout this? Let me latch the cow up." She hurried away and was back in a minute.

I followed her to the warmth of the kitchen where Polly was stirring something at the stove.

"Set that stew off a minute, Polly, we're goin' to the middle room."

The "middle room" was a bedroom, a sewing room and a living room all in one. Miss Rainey pulled a rocking chair close to the little grate glowing with red coals.

As the blue cold of my legs gave way to warmth, I was finding it hard to believe I was actually sitting in Miss Rainey's house.

Polly had followed us, wiping her hands on her apron. She was Miss Rainey's sister and almost fifteen years younger. She had come there to live after both her parents had died. In childhood she had had polio which left one leg shorter, giving her a stiff, rolling gait because she had to swing herself to and fro. She did the cooking and housework, while Miss Rainey did the yard work, including feeding the chickens, milking the cow and keeping the kindling box filled to start fires.

Polly stood behind the chair Miss Rainey had drawn up to the fire for her. Black wiry hair circled her crown and was braided so tightly that it looked cast in metal. Double rows of wire hairpins riveted it to her head. Polly's dark eyes were uncommunicative. She, too, had withdrawn from Miss Rainey because of the closing of the lane. It had shut out the only person in the world who had ever taken notice of Polly—Jepp Caudill, a bachelor who lived on the hill behind them.

It had started one summer day when Polly was stringing beans on the kitchen porch and he was walking through the lane near their gate. He'd smiled and said, "Good mornin' Miss Polly." Then he'd leaned against the gatepost for a minute as though he were tired. Polly got up, unlatched the gate and invited him to rest in the shade of the porch. She drew him a drink of cold water from the well. Thanking her, he pleasantly passed the time of day before going on his way. But now he seldom went out of the holler. With the creek to cross and the ridge too rocky, it was difficult for him to hunt and pick his steps with his wooden leg. Polly missed him and it was Miss Rainey's fault.

"Tell Polly 'bout Miss Kelly's cow."

I told about the cow not coming home and about everybody going to hunt for her. She listened. "When you say everbidy was huntin' for her, who was everbidy?" Miss Rainey asked.

"I don't know exactly," I told her uncertainly, as her eyes searched mine for a better answer.

"You see they's more to this tale. Why don't you come this way tomar' from school? They'll be a lot more to tell then, won't they, Polly?"

Polly didn't say.

That evening I told Mother that I was late coming home because Miss Rainey had invited me to call on her.

"Where on earth did you see Miss Rainey?"

"We just happened to meet. You should see her middle room, Mother. It's so pretty with blue paper tacked on the walls with headed tacks that go through the center of silver discs about the size of fifty-cent pieces. I imagine that in firelight the discs on the ceiling would twinkle like stars. She wants me to come by tomar' because it was so late we didn't get time to talk much."

"Well, tomar' why don't you ask her where she got that paper and how much it cost?" She was imagining too. Mother's mind could so easily be captured by dangling something pretty in front of her.

The next day I climbed that wall of debris and walked confidently to Miss Rainey's door. She opened it immediately and, calling to Polly, led us to the middle room, where she and I sat while Polly remained standing. After politely inquiring about my family, Miss Rainey leaned back and folded her arms. Then I told her, "They found Miss Kelly's cow. She fell over a cliff. They took her some cow feed and water because she's not able to walk home. Tomar' they will bring her home on a sled, and then to Nat Comb's slaughterhouse."

Taking in every word and leaning forward, she asked, "Which cliff was that?"

I pointed to her side of the mountain, "Back of the hill where the old mine used to be."

She picked up the poking stick and stirred the coals in the fire as she sat studying a minute. "That cow didn't go that fer by herself. That's why I closed off the lane— to keep blackguards out. You see now, Polly?"

Polly saw nothing but the blue tongues of flame licking at the huge lumps of coal. She turned and swung herself back to the kitchen.

"Now who took the feed and water to the cow?" Miss Rainey wanted to know.

"Well, I didn't get that part, but somebidy had to take it if it was took to her."

"Yes," she said, "somebidy had to take it, but who? Polly's makin' ginger cake tomar'. When you come, we'll all have a piece."

I asked her where Mother could buy the wallpaper. "It's called building paper," she said and going to the stand table between the beds she returned with a big Montgomery Ward catalog and laid it in my lap. "It's right here. You been to school. Write it down." When she gave me a penny pencil and a rough tablet, I wrote it all down, word for word, and read on and on in the catalog.

Mother was a little angry that I'd stayed so long, but was mollified by the directions I'd brought her for ordering the paper and very pleased to hear that enough to do the room would cost only three dollars, including the silver discs. I told her I'd write the order for her and that there were other things in the catalog I could write down. Mother had a better idea: "Ask Miss Rainey where we can get a catalog." Indeed I would, but not until I'd finished reading it at Miss Rainey's house.

The next day when I stopped, we didn't go to the middle room, but sat in the kitchen. Polly presided over the kitchen with its coal cook stove sitting cornerways, so the sometimes red-hot stove pipes wouldn't set the walls afire. And cornerways behind the stove was nailed a broomstick hung full of big circles of dried pumpkin resembling huge donuts threaded on a pole. Dried pumpkin was the main ingredient in Polly's "Forever and a Day" stew. She clipped off a ring of it and cut it into chunks as she stood over the stew pot. The stew gave off an earthy, pungent aroma as it mixed with ham hocks.

Getting out three saucers, Polly filled each with warm slices of ginger cake with dried apples between the layers. We sat at the table to eat it. Before Miss Rainey could mention the cow, I began, "Bessie Hughes told my mother that Lizzie Adams' daughter married a foreigner that she met at the carnival in Whitesburg."

"Upon my word," Miss Rainey exclaimed. "What country is he from?"

"New York. Way up in New York. He talks so fast they can't understand a word he says. The other day he was talking to Miss Adams about somebidy named Harold and Miss Adams said she thought he said "hair oil" and they got all mixed up. She says it takes about a year for New Yorkers to understand English."

"Listen to that, Polly." Miss Rainey turned to me, "What can you expect lettin' your daughters mix with total rank strangers?"

At last Miss Rainey got up from the table. I rose with her and followed her to the middle room. I now had unlimited freedom between our house and hers. She was so curious to hear all the news from the outside world and Mother was so curious to hear what Polly and Miss Rainey were doing, that I merely had to walk a sensitive line, not overstaying my welcome at each visit and not staying so long that Mother would be angry. I liked sitting by the fire with Miss Rainey, but I couldn't wait till she dismissed my "news reports" and went to the yard. She had accepted me as a family member, calling me "Honey," and designating one of the big rockers as "my chair."

The catalog was lying on my chair. She had noticed my interest in it and had thoughtfully placed it there. "Read as long as you want and mark your place with this." She handed me a heavy shoe lace. "And then when you come again, you'll know where you are." She picked up the poking stick to rearrange the fire and after putting a fresh lump of coal on it, she left the room to do her evening work. The sun fell behind the high mountain peaks in mid-afternoon, giving a long twilight called evening.

With Miss Rainey gone and Polly in the kitchen, I was alone in the big rocker near a warm glowing fire with the catalog in my lap. The catalog was from a fairy world. It had sets of dishes all matching, wallpaper, paint, dolls with lacy dresses, shoes and so many other things that it made Ali Baba's cave look empty. Underneath the things it was written that, with care, they wouldn't "chip, shrink or fade" and that the shoes were "long wearing."

On the stand table, a little round clock with four brass feet was ticking away in measured time. The long black rifle that hung over the fireboard was looking down protectively. I was lulled into a place where I'd never been before: a place called "Privacy." No orders were given here. No children were clinging to me. No teacher was standing over me. The little clock kept reassuring me that I was all alone, all alone, all alone.

"You can eat supper with us, can't you?" Miss Rainey startled me.

"Supper? Already?" I marked my place with the shoelace, thanked her with my regrets and hurried home.

I gave mother the recipe for Polly's ginger cake: "Take as much flour for as big a cake as you intend to make; pour on enough molasses till you can't hardly stir it; add one egg and a pinch of soda and a heap of ginger; then you pour buttermilk in it till it's as light and easy to stir as cornbread. But fore you start all this, pour boiling water over a few handfuls of dried apples and leave them till the cake is baked and cool, then put them between the layers with brown sugar sprinkled over them."

While I was giving Mother Polly's directions for the cake, she looked as though I was giving her a deep secret that no one in Corbin Glow, where we had come from, would ever know. The very next evening at supper we had a huge ginger cake, baked in the big rectangular cornbread pan. Cut in half, it made square instead of round layers. All during supper it decorated the center of the table. Father gave a surprised and very pleased look at Mother. It was the first dessert we'd ever had other than wild blackberry cobbler.

In the meantime, Miss Rainey was waiting impatiently for my next report and Miss Ervin, my teacher, was writing one big word in red letters across all my school assignments: CARELESS. Some of my sentences didn't begin with capitals and half of them didn't end with periods. In spite of these faults, I was very disappointed that Miss Ervin hadn't noticed all the new words from Montgomery Ward's catalog that I was putting between these unimportant things.

As my visits continued throughout the winter, Miss Rainey programmed them as tightly as any corporate executive's agenda. She opened the meetings with, "How's your family?" She only wanted one news report a day. "I need to study on it to see if hit's all there," she'd say.

"Sam Williams has just finished shocking his fodder on the ridge lot above the creek. He has thirty-five shocks," I told her.

"Thirty-five? He had forty there last year. What happened?" she asked.

"I don't know."

"Well, find out, honey. Five shocks short is a lot of fodder. He may have sold some of his livestock." I knew there was more to do on this story.

"Cindy Day is making a new quilt," I told her. "The pattern is Clay's Choice. It has six hundred pieces in it." I'd counted them myself.

"Clay's Choice? She has two Clay's Choices already. What's she want with another'n?" she asked.

"She said she likes Henry Clay and that she wants that quilt on all her beds."

"Henry Clay . . . yes, that's a fittin' choice."

"Miss Honeycutt is weaning her baby now," I reported.

"Baby? That child's fourteen months old. He must have a mouthful of teeth by this time."

"It looked like he only had four," I told her.

With my reports finished each day, Miss Rainey'd go to the barrel in the corner of the back room and take out a sweet potato wrapped in a page from an old catalog. She'd peel and slice it in cold, crisp discs oozing a sugary syrup and then serve it to me on a saucer. After she left the room, I'd be alone with the big catalog and the little clock.

One time later when I called on Miss Rainey, I was surprised to find a gentleman there. About thirty-five, he wore a gray striped suit with a very white shirt and a tie of gray silk with darker gray dots. He looked like he'd just stepped from the pages of the catalog and, as the people of Letcher would say, "He was the genuine article." Miss Rainey introduced me to her son by reminding him that his daddy had worked with my father.

"I remember Mr. Bailey. Dad liked him a lot."

"Tom is working with John L. Lewis. The miners are goin' to get a dollar a ton for loading coal, ain't they, Tom?"

"Maybe more." He smiled.

I couldn't wait for Father to come home that evening. Through the grapevine, everybody in Letcher had heard of John L. Lewis and he was looked upon by the miners as a savior who would deliver them from the mining overlords. The miners had already agreed among themselves to follow him to the death. Groups of them sitting around on railroad ties on Sunday evenings affectionately referred to him as "Ole John L." And they'd say, and it was the truth, that John L. wouldn't take any guff from these slave-driving operators.

I couldn't wait to tell Father that John L. had sent out one of his own men right here to Letcher. Wait till he heard this!

Father heard, then stuck a finger in my face. "I don't want this peddled to the four corners of Christendom, Miss Newspaper."

THE TELEGRAM

W e were all on the front porch in the early dusk that night when John Hughes stopped at our gate with a telegram. It had arrived in Blackey that morning, but the office there had to wait for somebody going to Letcher to deliver it. Father was weary from loading coal all day and now, as he read the telegram, the lines in his face deepend.

"This is what it says." He straightened up and in a strained voice read the telegram to all of us. Turning away, he added, "Yore grandfather's dyin'." Although we barely knew our grandfather, we all cried because we had never seen or heard such sadness in Father.

He looked into Mother's tear-filled face. "I'm leavin' tonight."

"The train don't run till three o'clock tomar'."

"I don't have money to buy a train ticket no matter what time it runs," he answered. And in bitterness he added, "They don't take Corbin Glow scrip. I'll catch the midnight freight out of here."

Except for the baby, nobody was put to bed that night. We all sat with Father in the kitchen. A little after ten o'clock we heard the train whistle blow mournfully as it moved through Letcher, hauling empty cars which would be exchanged for full ones in Corbin Glow. Mother tensed as the train clattered by, knowing that on its return trip Father would be trying to snatch a handhold in pitch blackness.

He asked Mother to put his clothes in a white cloth flour sack, explaining, "I have to throw 'em off the freight 'fore I jump off and then try to find 'em in the dark."

When she finished putting the clothes in the bag, she watched Father tie a big knot in its top half, for handhold. Then, convincing him to "eat a bite," she fried potatoes and eggs which he picked at half-heartedly just to please her.

Father looked at the clock, then, not being a kissing person, put his hands on our shoulders, each in turn and told us to be good until he got back. Mother kissed him at the door and watched as he stepped out into the darkness, tired, alone and heartbroken.

We all continued to sit in the kitchen—waiting, waiting expectantly until we heard it. The loneliest sound in the world, a midnight freight train sounding its melancholy whistle on a Kentucky curve. Mother held her breath as the train roared through Letcher, knowing that at that very moment Father would be grasping desperately for a car ladder. When the sound of the train died away, she sighed in deep resignation. "We're all in God's hands."

Father returned a week later, this time a paying passenger, since his brother had lent him the money. We learned that Grandfather had died at three o'clock the day he had arrived. When Mother heard this, she said to my father, "You see? It's a God's blessin' we had no money

that night or you'd a never seen your father alive agin." If
he had taken a passenger train, my father would have arrived too late.

LIE SHINGLES

He was called Lie Shingles. He was a beggarman who walked a two-week circuit up and down Rockhouse Creek on a route that he'd laid out so thoughtfully that he never had to ask for but one meal from the same family. Thus, he would have breakfast or supper with the same family every two weeks. He had been at this so long that he had picked the families he liked best and they accepted him. Many of them, as in Mother's case, eagerly looked forward to his coming. During the two coldest months of the winter he dropped out of sight. As far as anybody could see, he had no home and where he slept nights was his very own secret. The only personal thing known about him was from Becky Browning, who confided, "Wuz him washing his shirt in the creek." His hair was thick and white and he kept it cut to just above his collar. He was about six feet tall, including his stoop, with deep lines in his face and intense warmth in his blue eyes.

Other beggarmen went to the back door and offered to draw water for the wash or chop kindling for the fire in exchange for the food they requested. But Lie Shingles offered to do nothing. Furthermore, the old, black split-tailed parson's coat he wore, even on the hottest days, gave him the privilege of knocking on the front door like a gentleman calling.

"Has yore family had breakfast, Madam?" he would inquire politely of Mother.

"Yes," she'd nod.

"Was there any little thing left, good woman?"

"Yes," Mother would nod, even though there had been nothing left but two or three biscuits. Inviting him to the kitchen, she would fry bacon and two eggs (or whatever we had in the house) and warm up the biscuits and coffee. Then, ushering the children out of the kitchen, she would tell them, out of his hearing, "You're not goin' to set there and stare at that pore man while he eats." When Lie Shingles finished his meal, he would thank Mother with a courtly bow.

One year in early May, Preacher Bennington told the people that he had heard word from the undertaker in Whitesburg that Lie Shingles had died and had asked to be buried in Letcher. He went on to say that as minister he would "be sayin' a few words at the funeral." Even though Lie Shingles had never been known to set foot in a church, the members all gathered under the big elm tree in the graveyard to sing their sad songs of remembrance and regret.

A few weeks later, on Decoration Day, the last Sunday in May, Mother put together a bouquet of flowers specially gathered from the edge of the woods to put on his grave. She carried the flowers and an old flour scoop for making a hole in the soft earth to hold the glass jar. I carried the bouquet. From a short distance in the cemetery we could see a new tombstone at his grave. Mother walked toward it while I went to the creek to fill the jar with water.

I came up to the grave and looked at the stone. I couldn't believe my eyes. There in deeply chiseled letters was printed ELISHA INGLES. I ran my fingers underneath the writing. "It says here, Mother, E-LI-SHA ING-LES." I took special care to pronounce each syllable.

"Yes. Lie Shingles. He called me a Good Woman."

THE PARLOR ORGAN

Spring had come to Letcher, whose wide-flung boundaries were almost indefinable. Two mountains merged into a low saddle, creating a protective semicircle at one end. A ridge with houses on it ran alongside Crase's Branch. This drained the two mountains and emptied into Rockhouse Creek, which then flowed into a long sweeping curve of the Kentucky River a mile or two on down the road.

Spring had come early this year. The color of the rocks on the mountains had turned from charcoal to steel blue. Their sharp edges had begun to soften, with green tufts of poke, plantain, and stickweed which mingled with the grasses around them. The ash tree in our front yard was leafing out, making a soft metallic sound against a breeze. Cold water streamed from the mountains, coming down every little gully, filling the creek to the very top of its rock-shelved banks, and here and there overflowing. Along the creek the big trunks were wet and black with sap running down the grooves in the rough bark.

When I left the house, I wasn't going anyplace, just walking, just walking up the creek, staying on the muddy path till the creek got on it, then moving off into the wet weeds, sometimes climbing through a fence to get away from a deepening, headlong swirl. I walked to the very head of the creek where three small streams merged in a low spot at the foot of the mountain. Here the creek's name was Crase's Branch and here was where Jim and Becky Hayes lived.

Becky was a stranger, but everybody knew all about her by now, for Jim's tragedy and romance had been talked about all winter long at every fireside.

His first wife, Suri, had died winter before last, a few months before her fifty-first birthday. Jim had gone back to Morgan County for another wife. He had been born and raised there and now made yearly trips back in a wagon to bring molasses to Letcher to sell. When he had gone the previous fall, he brought Becky back with him, married.

The people weren't taking to his new wife as well as Jim was. "She can't hold a candle to Suri," they said.

Suri had been tall and thin, but not willowy. She was too straight and stiff. Her hair had been white for so long that few could remember what color it had been. She held high recognition from the people because she followed exactly their codes of religious principles. When the preacher at the Church of God called for testimonies at the services, Suri, unlike many, never had to confess any sinful thought or missteps, for she never made any missteps. Conversation in her house was Biblical. Singing in her house was churchly. The preacher's praises of her rang up and down the holler. She was held in awe as a saint.

Now, here Jim had come home one day with Becky—a "heathern" as far as the church was concerned, her name on no roll. It was said that, "she can make a guitar talk" and that she played and sang ditties and jugs with Jim on the fiddle. It was also said that she helped him carry his whiskey to the house from the barn, where he had kept it out of sight for years.

The Preacher didn't go to the head of the holler anymore. It was agreed by the nodding of heads around firesides that winter that "Jim has bartered his soul for Becky."

I stopped at a pole bridge that lay across the creek, a huge log with the rough bark left on it. The path dwindled out a little way farther at a barn. It didn't go over the mountain, since there was nothing on the other side to go to. I looked across the creek to a house. Few people would stop there to ask for a drink of water or to rest in the shade for a minute.

"Come over." Becky stepped from behind the gate. Calling like that from Jim's yard, it had to be Becky. As I skimmed over the log, which ended exactly at the entrance, she opened the gate wide. Leaping off into the yard, I could see mud oozing between her toes. I was fourteen and she didn't look much older. Her hair, about the color of a twist of Red-Ox Tobacco, maybe a little lighter, was pulled back into a low careless coil. She wore a pink flowered dress hanging loose. The belt was no doubt on a nail somewhere in the house.

"You live close to here?" she asked softly.

"Not too close," and I gave her my name.

"I'm Jim's wife, Becky. His new wife," she added with a laugh. I could see she was dying for company as she reached for my hand. "You can stop a minute?" Still holding it, she led me across to the back yard.

A well was near the porch. Its unpainted, weathered wooden box was so old that it had the texture of woven cloth that had been dipped in pale blue dye, with streaks of white here and there where the dye hadn't taken. Behind the well, running uphill, was a row of bee gums, gum trees with beehives in them. On up the hill was a chicken house of the same color. The mountain, rising above the yard, was lit with snowy petals, the pale green leaves of dogwood trees and the rosy bouquets of redbuds.

"I was fixin' to do my churnin'," Becky said, smiling.

As I wiped the mud from my bare feet onto an old coffee sack on the porch, Becky came from the well with a gourd full of water which she graciously poured over my feet. We stepped into the kitchen. Its unpainted walls were made of the same pine lumber as the floor. The ceiling was made of this same pine, although it was smoother and put together more tightly. It was smoked as black as the iron coal stove that sat cornerways.

On the back of the stove, directly over the little iron reservoir, sat a churn of milk covered with a dish. Becky lifted the dish and swarped her forefinger through the clabbered milk. Satisfied that it was thick enough to churn, she licked her finger clean; then, pouring a dipper of cold water over a wooden dasher, she dropped it into the churn. On a nail behind the stove hung a brown earthenware lid with a hole in the center. Becky slid it down over the long handle of the dasher.

"Suri's dasher is way too long for me and I hate brown churns." Her voice was full of forbearance. Then she burst into a dimpled laugh and gestured toward a door on the opposite wall. "I do the churnin' in the dinin' room, chairs in there." She picked up the churn and went through the doorway.

Following, I stopped dead in my tracks on the threshold, for there, cornerways in the big room, sat an old parlor organ. Never had I dreamed that wood could lend itself to such goings-on. The oak had been carved into every conceivable design and pattern, decorated with spools, spindles and spires. A looking glass hung in the center, surrounded by little corner shelves. Each shelf dripped a semi-circle of lace from a crocheted doily. On the doilies sat pink crepe paper roses in glass jars painted blue. Huge red roses were woven into the carpet that covered the organ's treadles on the floor and right before my eyes, on a ledge of scalloped and beaded oak, leaned a songbook.

Becky had set the churn on the floor and had pulled two chairs from the table when she noticed that I was "overtook" by the organ. "Play a piece," she invited. I moved closer to the organ, staring at the rows of stops capped in snowy disks of ivory, each with a black symbol written on it in Old English script that I couldn't even read. "I've never seen one except in a picture."

Becky laughed, "Well, name somethin' you want to hear."

After spreading a clean white cloth around the churn dasher to keep the flies away, she came over to show me how it was played. She sat down on the round matching stool with its three legs which were pinched into rings, turned into balls, and ended in three swirled globes of green glass feet. Facing me she sat down, and the stool whirled her to face the organ.

Again she asked for a title and I named "Pretty Polly." It was a favorite Letcher County ballad about a beautiful young girl who was murdered by a jilted suitor on Pine Mountain on her wedding day. The organ began a mournful dirge. Becky's voice moved into the music in weeping tones of low minor keys:

Polly, pretty Polly, come go along with me.
Polly, pretty Polly, come go along with me.
Before you get married some pleasure to see.

He led her over mountains and valleys so deep.
He led her over mountains and valleys so deep.
At last pretty Polly began to mourn and to weep.

William, sweet William, please spare me my life.
William, sweet William, please spare me my life.
And I will be-ee your own loving wife.

The song went on to tell that Polly was buried and her jilted suitor was hanged. As the funereal tones of the organ slowly died away, I was almost in tears. I had never heard such sad music in my whole life. Becky hummed a minute, pushing down a key here and there, and then she began singing "The Little Rosewood Casket" in a voice of total despair. The organ softly followed in sobbing notes:

There's a little rosewood casket
Sitting on a marble stand.

In it's a packet of love letters
Written by my true love's hand.

Go and bring them to me, sister
And sit here upon my bed.
And read them over and over
Till my aching heart grows dead.

Every song I'd ever heard, Becky could play. And when a chord reached out and pulled me in, I began singing with her. We sang on and on till she suddenly stopped and, whirling on the stool to face me, said she'd like to sell the organ for five dollars to help buy a new guitar.

The possibility of owning this treasure struck me with such force that I couldn't breathe. I didn't need to breathe.

"I'll buy it!"

I dashed out through the kitchen with Becky's voice calling after me, "Come back!"

I couldn't wait to get home. I skimmed the tree trunk over the creek and slid down the muddy bank onto the path that I had plodded up so aimlessly. I didn't have time to unravel the path that was half covered with water. I flowed with the creek which ran now with me, now beside me, and now behind me. Leaping from stone to stone, I'd miss one and plunge into the water to my knees. Minnows fanned out in every direction.

My heart was beating to the steady rhythm of the organ—the wind was blowing with it, the clouds were moving with it, the creek was flowing with it. The whole world was moving to the chords of that beautiful organ.

I ran through the gate and leaped onto the back porch where Mother and Father were sitting.

"Becky Hayes wants to sell her organ," I panted, facing Mother.

"Suri's organ?" She couldn't believe this.

"Becky's organ now," I corrected.

"How much does she want for it?"

"Only five dollars."

"Lord save us all, she wants enough."

I dropped limply to the floor beside her chair. "I'll die without that organ. I declare, Mother, I can't live without it."

She looked down at my pleading face with a flicker of sympathy. "I'll have to think about it." She glanced at Father.

"No use to think," he said brusquely. "Organ music is too dry, and organs were made with the pure idle in mind."

"I've knowed some hardworking Christian women that played the organ," Mother bristled. "And I promise not a thing'll let be gone undone. The law'll be laid down afore that organ ever sets foot in this house." She was bargaining now.

"Coal miners don't make money and you know it." he said firmly. "Where you goin' to get five dollars?"

"Some*wheres*."

"We just ain't got it, Laura." He got up and left the porch. After he'd gone, I told Mother all about the organ.

"And ask Becky to throw in the crepe-paper flowers and the doilies that are on it."

"We've got no organ yet to put doilies on yet." She came down heavily on the word "yet." Adding, "But I'll look into it."

Next morning Mother combed her hair earlier than usual. Undoing the one long braid she slept in, she combed it smooth, twisted it into a long rope and knotted it at the back of her head. She put on a clean starched and ironed apron, tying the strings into a perfect bow at the back. Then she set forth to see Becky.

I followed her to the gate where she stopped and said to me, "Don't let the children in sight of that well, and keep the baby on the porch out of the sun. . . ."

"Yes, yes," I interrupted impatiently. "Go on, Mother, go on."

My two oldest brothers were able to go off and play by themselves. I brought the other children to the front yard away from the well. The youngest ones played on the front porch, which had a two-foot-high enclosure of chicken wire fence around it to keep them from falling from its seven-foot height. When a fight broke out among the children, I quoted Mother exactly: "I'll get the keenest switch from the cherry tree and stripe your legs." If only she'd get home. . . .

The agonizing wait finally ended when I saw Mother leave the creek path and come up the hill toward the house. I grabbed the baby from the porch floor and ran to meet her. He held out both hands and she took him in her arms. "Are the children all right?" she asked before I could open my mouth.

"Yes, yes. What did Becky say?"

"She said Jim'll bring the organ as soon as the creek goes down."

My heart was beating so wildly that I could only gasp, "How did you get it?"

"I swapped her ten of them big dommer hens."

"Hens?" My mind had been so locked onto dollars that I had thought of nothing but cash.

"Your father didn't mention hens, he only mentioned money."

When we had reached the gate, I dashed across the yard, up the steps, across the porch and into the front of the house. It had only three rooms, two across the front and the kitchen in back. The front rooms each had two double beds and a baby crib, two windows, a coal-burning iron gate and a big door leading to a wide veranda, which was our living room most of the year. The rooms were full to overflowing.

I ran out of the house and into Mother crossing the porch. "We have to put the organ across this door, it won't fit anywhere else." I flung my arm toward the wide door with the glass panel.

She stepped inside and studied the rooms from the threshold between them. "Yes, but we'll have to cut a narrow door on that wall to the back porch." She indicated the room whose door I was closing.

Day in and day out, for what seemed a thousand years, I watched the level of the creek, inch by inch. Finally, on the third day as the sun came up, I could see the path by the creek. It lay uncovered, dark and flat beside the shining water.

Soon we saw Jim coming. He had the organ sitting upright in an old homemade sled with thick hickory runners. A big white dappled horse was pulling it. Brown sticky mud clung to horse, sled and Jim. The organ, like a rich Victorian lady going for a ride, sat primly facing the driver. The lacy doilies tacked to the little shelves, and the bouquet of crepe-paper roses tied to a spindle, fluttered with each lurch of the sled and made it seem that she was waving to an admiring crowd.

The looking glass in the center of the organ was, in turn, picturing everything. Now the clouds, now the creek, now Jim and finally our gateposts. . . .

I breathed a sigh of total exhaustion.

GIDEON

A stranger wouldn't have climbed the cliff, but Gideon was no stranger here. Most of his forty years had been spent wading creeks, climbing mountains and digging coal up one holler and down the other. He knew every inch of this country whose creeks and riverbeds were its mapped roads and paths as well as he knew his own back yard.

Standing on the railroad track, he looked up at the cliff with some respect and not a little gratitude, for climbing it would cut a mile and a half off his journey. He had already been walking four miles to get home before church. He had preached the night before at a revival meeting up on Rockhouse Creek, had stayed the night with friends and was now on his way home to Letcher.

Gideon sat down on the end of a railroad tie and took off his heavy brogans. Tying the shoes together with the rawhide strings and flinging them over his shoulder, he let his bare feet find the narrow ledges here and there leading upward on the rock. The cliff was so precarious that Gideon hardly dared to breathe, but at last he reached the little path at the top that only the most adventuresome traveled. He sat down to put the heavy cowhide shoes on and then hurried on toward home.

That summer Gideon was the preacher at the morning services of the Church of God, an unpainted, abandoned school house that sat all alone on Green Knob. He had no Divinity School training and while he could read well enough, he'd never been taught to write, except his name. But once he had read a passage in the Bible, it never slipped his mind. He felt that God had called him to preach here and lead these people out of despair.

At one end of the church a podium had been raised. This platform was lined with benches where the "born again" members sat, and in its center was located a lectern sawed from lumber that was never painted. This simple, enforced frugality was echoed in other ways.

The visiting preachers brought their own Bibles and the people provided their own music. Since there was no organ or piano, Gideon told the people that they could "make a joyful noise unto the Lord" with their guitars, banjos and violins, so they did. They had put a lot of the old Bible tales to rhyme and music and had learned them by heart. Gideon also told them, "If all you've got to give is Corbin Glow scrip, God will accept it. It will buy coal to heat the house of the Lord."

Gideon was soon known far and wide as a man of God and people came from all over to hear him preach and to hear the music in his church. When he walked to the lectern of a Sunday morning, a hush would fall over the room as the congregation studied his impressive bearing. He was over six feet tall. He dressed in denim overalls with the big brass latches on his galluses fastened high over a white shirt. He cut his own thick dark hair, squaring it off in front with bangs and letting it come down straight from the sides so that it appeared that he was wearing a helmet. He had only one eye, the other having been blown out by dynamite in the mines. As he preached, he would cock his head from side to side with the muscular movements of a bird.

His height, his helmeted head and the big red empty socket gave him a fearsome, even awesome appearance as he strode to the lectern with the Bible in his hand to bring "a message straight from God." Indeed he looked like a warrior who had just descended the mountain after being locked in mortal combat with some evil entity. The people paid close attention to every word he said.

"Your overalls may be patched, the flowers on your dresses may be faded, but God wants you to know that fine clothes is not what he's goin' to judge you on, brothers and sisters."

"No, Lord," the congregation responded.

Each Sunday, taking his sermons from the red letters written in the New Testament, Gideon brought them a message of hope and assurance. "Lay not up for yourselves treasures upon Earth where moth and rust doth corrupt." Turning from the printed word, he added, "The Lord knows that we have no treasures to lay up, but he wrote this for us not to covet treasures and not to feel poor because we don't have any. We lay up our treasures in Heaven by believing in Him."

"Amen."

The theology that stood between the members and the grave was either black or white and beyond was

Heaven or Hell and while on Earth they were resigned to their lot of "just passin' through."

"Take no thought for your life, what ye shall eat or what ye shall drink . . . nor yet what ye shall put on."

"No, Lord."

"Therefore, take no thought saying 'What shall we eat, what shall we drink, or wherewithal shall we be clothed?' The Lord will feed us and he will clothe us. We need only to believe in Him."

"Amen."

Gideon looked out on the congregation at the men in patched overalls and saw their work-worn calloused hands; he saw the women in their faded, cheap cotton dresses with their weary hands folded in their laps.

"The foxes have holes and the birds of the air have nests; but the Son of Man hath nowhere to lay his head. Should we not be thankful that we have a roof over our heads?" Gideon asked them.

"Yes, Lord."

"Verily, I say unto you that a rich man shall hardly enter the Kingdom of Heaven."

"Amen."

"For what hath man advantaged if he gain the whole world and be cast away?"

"Nothing, Lord," the people answered.

When we returned home after church, Mother would make little balls of biscuit dough and drop them into the big pot of chicken she had left cooking on the back of the stove. They sank to the bottom and when they floated back to the surface, they were huge, light dumplings. Father offered grace: "Lord, bless the hands that prepared this food and bless those that labored for it and bless it to the use of our bodies. Amen."

Gideon was our nearest neighbor when we moved to Letcher. His rented two-room house with a long front porch that was at least ten feet off the ground, sat across the creek from ours at the end of a lane bordering an apple orchard. He had helped us unload our belongings that Sunday afternoon when we first arrived.

He washed his own clothes, flinging them over the wire fence to dry. Sometimes in winter he draped a pair of overalls over the back of a chair, then pulled it close to the fire to dry them faster, making his whole house smell like Fels-Naptha soap. On days there was no work, he patched and mended his clothes, sewing on buttons with long strands of #8 linen thread.

Mother would often give me a big piece of fresh baked cornbread or a bowl of chicken and dumplings to take to Gideon and I would sit with him while he ate it. Then he would wash the dish for me to take home. Handing it to me he would laugh, "If I don't send this right back, she won't have nothin' to send me any more in."

I was fascinated with Gideon's house. It changed its color with the ease of a chameleon. It was made of wide unpainted boards running up and down with narrow ones to batten the cracks. On a clear day in April all the window panes would be blue, and the shadows running up the sides of the battens would be blue too, coloring the whole house as blue as the sky. August bleached it to dry bones of dead white. When the rains of November came, the little house took on a somber gray look. Its glistening wet roof was a more intense shade of this same gray and the smoke that the rain tried to beat back into the chimney was a dark black gray. And then, some days, the sun would come out and the gray would turn to pearl, bright and shiny pearl.

One Spring there was a great surge of activity at Gideon's house. The whole fence along his lane was hung with washed sheets, blankets and quilts. He picked up twigs and branches from his property and burned them. He pulled the weeds away from the gateposts and from the edge of his path and he cleaned all the windows until they sparkled. Mother, looking that way, asked, "What on earth?"

Two days later when the Corbin Glow coal truck dumped Gideon's coal at the foot of our hill because it couldn't get up his narrow path, he came to carry it home in sacks. It was then he told us he was getting married.

Sitting on the porch, he told us all, "I finally found the perfect woman when I helped Brother Spencer in his revival on Rockhouse Creek. She don't hanker to rule or run nothin'. She don't tell nobody what to do or when to do it."

Not until he married had Gideon ever owned anything that needed witnessing and signing to make it legally his. Now, a week later, he slowly printed his name on his marriage certificate. He brought Louizy to church that Sunday to meet everybody.

She was twenty years younger than Gideon, wispy, with dark hair and a passive sweet face. Her expansive cheekbones looked like nothing more than bony brackets to hold the big, brown gentle eyes from which she stared in submissive innocence. The whole community loved her.

When we got home after church, Father said, "Well, I guess Gideon has found one woman in a million."

"She's not that pretty," said Mother.

"No, but she don't rattle on and on about somethin' she knows nothing about, I noticed."

With deep contentment Gideon settled into the masculine habits of heads of households. Louizy, the perfect wife, picked wild blackberries and made jam for the buttermilk biscuits Gideon liked for breakfast. His coffee was served after the milk was stirred into it. His shirts were held open ready for his arms to slip into the sleeves, and then Louizy buttoned them for him and he'd thank her with a little kiss on the forehead. He never needed to raise his voice, for there was nothing to command.

Then the baby came. Like a blossom fallen from one of the wild apple trees, he was pink and white, with blue sky in his eyes and the golden sunset in his hair. He was part and parcel of the little plot of earth on which he had been born.

Gideon slowly and grudgingly found that part of his claim on Louizy had loosened. Indeed, her soft words and gentle concern now seemed all for the baby. But Gideon decided to tolerate this. The sudden neglect had already been partly compensated for by the pride he felt watching Louizy show the baby to the Letcher mothers who came to admire him from the time he was three days old. By the baby's third week, when Louizy carried him to the rocker at the hearth to nurse him, Gideon felt drawn into the curious aura that was a family. Leaning toward his child, his great paw-like hand attempted to wipe the beads of sweat from the nursing baby's brow.

Louizy was soon back into the days of normal activity, except that the baby was always with her. Again able to join Gideon at church, she dressed the baby with great care in his best finery, a little shirred cap and ruffled booties, and carrying him under a big black umbrella to keep the sun off him, they'd go to the church on Green Knob.

The church that had been built as a schoolhouse was still bare of any religious symbols. The narrow back end of the long rectangular building sat on stones embedded in the ribs of the mountain. As the building left the ground at the back, the props grew higher. Front steps with no risers went up to a landing, turned and climbed on to the front door. The membership of this church at first was sparse. Usually, they who called themselves "Saints" sat on the podium facing the congregation, but in winter, Saints and Sinners alike gathered around the big iron coal stove which sat in the center of the room.

One night at a prayer meeting, Louizy, having no part in the service, seated herself down below facing the podium beside her neighbors, Orb Whitaker and his wife. The meeting began with a song joyously sung to the rhythmic strumming of a guitar, clapping hands and tapping feet. After a few songs, testimonies of faith were called for. As Brother Orb stood to testify for the Lord, he loomed directly over the baby, who began to scream.

Louizy quickly unbuttoned her bodice to hush him with her breast, as was instinctively done to quiet all babies in Letcher, and ordinarily no attention was paid to this act, but Gideon, who had paid no mind to this ritual by other mothers, was struck deaf as he watched every eye shift from Brother Orb to Louizy. Their attention to her had been drawn only by the baby's cries, but Gideon sat breathing heavily, while his confusion grew into ponderous, jealous anger. He did not rise to make the Altar Call, which was his duty, nor when the meeting was over did he shake hands with any warmth. Picking up the lantern he'd left by the door, he lit it and led Louizy, carrying the baby, down the church steps. The lantern's glow lighted her footsteps along the path and gave movement to the fringy, shadowy weeds as they walked in silence.

What followed when Gideon arrived home that night wasn't known till Louizy came to church on Sunday. Knowing how Gideon sat when he sewed and recognizing his big loose stitches, I clearly saw him in my mind's eye doing it. So clearly did I see him that I told Mother exactly how he did it.

When they got home, he set the lantern high on the mantel and paid the proper attention to seeing Louizy and the baby to bed and asleep. Setting himself in a rocker at the hearth, Gideon stared into the cold, dead ashes in the grate and saw all those heads in church turn toward Louizy. Suddenly he moved the lantern to a chair beside his rocker and walked over to the nail on which Louizy hung her two dresses. Lifting them off, he picked up the scissors from the mantel and cut two slits up and down in each bodice, slits that her breasts would contour into round openings when put through to nurse the baby. With his one eye turned toward the light, he held a needle close as he threaded it and then set about to hem the slits in the sturdy backstitch he used to mend his clothes. From time to time as he worked, he turned the wick of the lantern higher.

Sitting close, with legs crossed and the cloth propped on his knee nearest the light, he worked intently, plucking the thread in and out as delicately as his calloused hands would allow, used as they were to pick and shovel. Going back and forth to the quilt scrap box, he found remnants of colorful cloth that he cut into rectangles to sew over and above the slits. He sewed buttons at the bottom of the slits to keep the flaps fastened down when they were not needed.

The lantern had burned low, the thread had knotted here and there, and the needle had made a red welt on the forefinger of his right hand when he finally held up the finished dresses to examine his handiwork. He was very pleased. In fact, he was so pleased that he decided to get his own breakfast and let Louizy and the baby sleep. While he hadn't had much sleep as he trudged the three miles to Corbin Glow mines, his step was light and his mind was overwhelmed at the wonder of his deed.

The next Sunday in church, although the flaps on Louizy's bodice didn't match the fabric of her dress and the stitching left much to be desired, she sat serenely throughout the service. When she nursed the baby, his little face was hidden by a flap of cloth with green and yellow sprigs on it. Gideon was preaching that day and when her eyes met his, she gave him a gentle smile.

KIN

Age, like hoarfrost that creeps into a garden on a fall night, touching but not quite killing, had touched Kin Walters the ploughman. No longer could his legs hold out to follow the plow through the long furrows from sunup to sundown. No longer could his booming voice command the mule, for it had cracked and thinned till he could barely lift it. The light in his eyes had dimmed till the silvery thread of the creek winding through the mountain was all that he could clearly see.

Now he sat on his porch in the twilight picking out the most desolate places in a desolate landscape: bare places, shaded places, dark and vague places. His hopes, like his crops when winter came, were now "laid by." His eyes, which had followed the creek through these mountains throughout his long life, followed it that night for the last time.

He walked out slowly and hooked the gate shut. He hushed the dog barking from under the porch floor; then after preparing himself for bed, he blew out the coal oil lamp.

Nature had made the rocks, mountains, and creeks, and over long generations had blended them with the people until they were one. Kin's house, set humbly halfway up the mountain, had three rough rooms and a great chimney. The chimney was made of flat stones laid on top of each other with yellow clay between. It couldn't be determined from looking at it whether the house had been built first and the chimney added, or whether the chimney had been made and the house attached to it. A path, beaten to a hard smoothness by rain and footsteps, led from the creek at the foot of the mountain to Kin's gate. It wound white and glistening along the mountainside.

High off the ground and clinging almost hopelessly to the house was a front porch. The saplings used for underpinnings fought a losing battle with erosion. On the porch sat two oak chairs, handmade by an old man on the other side of the mountain, with ladder backs and hickory splint bottoms. The curved ladder parts were set in by wooden dowels whittled by hand. The chairs, stained with walnut juice, sold for fifty cents apiece. When he married, Kin had bought four. When he died, two of them facing each other four feet apart would be the bier for his pine coffin.

Kin had been a plowman. He plowed cornfields, tobacco and potato patches all up and down the river. When my brother and I walked to Elk Creek to ask Kin when he could plow for us (we were already on his list), he would answer, "I think I can do it, maybe around Monday." He'd lift his eyes in a level gaze, adding, "If nothin' takes place 'tween now and then." Or sometimes he'd amend this to "then."

When Monday came, if it didn't rain, Kin's bare feet would be following a freshly plowed furrow that grew from a thin brown line to a rectangle and on into a soft brown square that would be our garden. He'd always stay overnight with us; it was too far to take his plow and mule back to Elk Creek before dark. Mother would make a pallet of old quilts on the floor for my brothers and give Kin their bed. She would have a good supper for Kin, and for breakfast we'd have fried chicken or ham and biscuits.

While he plowed, one of my younger brothers was his assigned waterboy. He'd sit in the shade till Kin hollered for a drink, then run to the well and draw a cold bucket of water. After drinking a few dippersful, Kin would turn the bucket upside down and pour cool water over his hot bare feet. Refreshed, he would wipe his great black moustache dry on his sleeve and, taking hold of the plow handles, speak coaxingly to his mule.

The minute a mountain flung a shadow over his work, Kin stopped plowing and unhitched his mule. He stopped earlier than other plowmen, but it was tolerated by everybody because Kin could sing. Early on the day he arrived, Mother would send children in all directions to tell the people that Kin would be singing on our porch that night. At eventide, on the little paths along creeks and ridges, would flow streams of people carrying unlit lanterns to light them home later.

In another time and another place, a cowherd who could neither read nor write became the "Father of English Poetry" when he answered the call of a voice: "Caedmon, sing me a song."

"What shall I sing?"

"Sing of the beginning of things."

Kin the plowman, who could neither read nor write, had surely obeyed a voice that called: "Kin, sing me a song."

"What shall I sing?"

"Sing of the ending of things."

Kin had a highly stylized way of singing. Sitting forward, head held sideways with his elbow resting on his knee and his chin in his palm, much like the statue of "The Thinker," he'd sing with his eyes closed. It was the mood of the songs that drew the people to listen. Like choruses from ancient Greek tragedies, they all dealt with death. His voice, which seemed to be coming from another time and another place, drew his hearers downward into an abyss of sorrow. No scenery in ancient Greece could present a better backdrop than these rocky, rugged crags that profiled the plowman as he sang in the shadowy twilight of our porch. No music ever written was lonelier than the whippoorwill cries woven mournfully through his songs. Kin cleared his throat and silence fell as he began to sing:

> In a dreary Yankee prison
> Where this Rebel prisoner lay,
> By his side there stood a Preacher,
> As his soul shall pass away.
> And he faintly whispered, "Parson,"
> As he clutched him by the hand,
> "Oh, Parson, tell me quickly,
> Will my soul pass through the Southland?"

As the tale in the plowman's song began to unfold, Miss Johnson took out her handkerchief and dabbed at her eyes. She was recalling vividly another scene her grandmother had witnessed: the Yankees burning her family's crops, leading off their horses, then shooting the dog and throwing him in their well. Her grandmother was so shocked by their incivility that she sat in a rocker and never spoke another word in her life. But Miss Johnson had come to hear Kin sing this song once more. It alone had the power to make her weep.

> Will my soul pass through the Southland,
> Through the old Virginia ground?
> Will I see the hills of Georgia
> And the green fields of Alabam?
> Will I see then the little Church House
> Where I placed my heart and hand?
> Oh, Parson, tell me quickly,
> Will my soul pass through the Southland?

The aging, cadaverous Clell Reynolds, listening intently to Kin's song, remembered more about the deadly aftermath of the Civil War than he did of the two brief years of sporadic fighting in this region. Kentucky's allegiance to the Union was so divided that family clans, in-laws, and neighbors were fighting one another. Firmly planted in this hostile and bitter battleground in the mountains of Kentucky were the roots of the deadly feuds that Clell, even now, was caught up in.

> Was for lovin' dear old Dixie
> In this cheerless cell I die.
> Was for lovin' dear old Dixie
> In this Northern state I die.
> Will you see my little daughter,
> Will you make her understand?
> Oh, Parson, tell me quickly
> Will my soul pass through the Southland?"

When the night air got too cool to sit in, the people would all shake hands with Kin, light their lanterns and wend their way home through the fallen dew. The night was sad, the people were sad, and sad were the songs the plowman sang.

Now, word had come that Kin was dead. Night had fallen on him with a hollow coldness. When daylight came that morning, Mr. Whitt, the carpenter on Elk Creek, was in his back yard making the coffin. It wasn't very deep, made of new pine boards shaped broad at one end and tapered toward the other. With a tiny tack hammer and brass springs such as shoemakers use, Mr. Whitt covered it inside and out with thin black cotton cloth. The sun had climbed only a short way when he pushed his wheelbarrow, the coffin riding crossways on top, up the mountain. And at one o'clock that day in June, the coffin, now bearing its sorrowful load, was carried down the mountain and up the railroad to the cemetery, a level place about two miles away. The people followed close behind in single file, or, when the road widened, in clusters, their heads bent low against the sun. Almost without pausing a step, and out of pure habit, some of the women picked a few wildflowers here and there, and as they walked they arranged and rearranged them.

The graveyard was on a slight knoll underneath a huge oak tree. To the deepest shade they bore the coffin and set it on two flat rocks. Fresh yellow earth with a lot of clay in it was piled in a mound at the side of the open grave. The dirt was damp and raw in the sunlight. The people turned their backs on it, facing the coffin under the tree. The women laid the flowers on the coffin lid, their colors

shining like jewels on the black cloth. Kin's favorite song
was sung in choked voices:

> The day is past and gone,
> The evening shades appear;
>
> O, may we all remember well
> The night of death is near.
>
> Lord, keep us safe this night,
> Secure from all our fears;
> May angels guard us while we sleep
> Till morning light appears.

When the song was finished, Brother Gideon, wearing a white shirt with bibbed overalls and heavy work
shoes, stepped from the semicircle formed by the people
and went to the trunk of the tree, where he turned to face
them. Under the tree, Gideon's shadowed face looked
chiseled in rock. At the beginning of his long sermon he
reminded the people how transitory life is, and at the end
of it, with a sweep of his hand toward the coffin, he showed
them how little could be taken to their final abode. The
people's eyes followed the sweep of his hand and saw the
golden bees that had come to the flowers on the black
cloth.

The shade under the tree had moved by the time the
preaching stopped, and the people began singing one last
tribute to the Plowman.

> We lay our garments by,
> Upon our beds to rest.

So Death will soon disrobe us all
Of what we here possess.

Mr. Whitt had stepped forward with a hammer and kneeling on one knee began to drive in the nails that had been set in the coffin lid. The sound of the hammer hitting the nails rang through the words of the song with a deadly finality. It sent the bees from the flowers, and it stilled the birds as it echoed from hill to mountain.

That night Kin's gate stood unlatched and open. No one could bear to shut him out so soon.

THIS SUN'S TOO HOT

The bare cupboards and cold stoves had taken the heart out of the people. The gentleness had faded from their eyes, and the softness had gone from their voices. A silence as hard and cold as the frozen creeks at the foot of the hills had settled over them that winter. The Depression had struck here, not with sudden shocking force, but rather like a disease that had gone undetected until there was no hope.

Now the mines had been shut down and the company had folded; the commissary stood empty and the electricity had been shut off. The great tipple that filled the train's gondolas with coal lay silent, and most of the houses in the mining camp were empty. Only the people who owned their homes had stayed that winter.

Father, hoping to stave off another winter like the one we'd just had, had staked off a piece of mountain belonging to the coal company. After clearing away the brush and stumps with the help of my three brothers, he'd hired a plowman to prepare the huge field. He bought the seeds from J. T. Browning's store on credit, promising to repay in corn, which was the staff of life there. Corn could be stone ground and, with buttermilk added, made into delicious cornbread. It would also feed the chickens, while the fodder would feed the cows.

He bought sweet potato slips from Miss Rainey who grew them in the early Spring in beds made of two-by-fours and covered them with old curtains to keep out the frost. They grew under the wispy shade of peach trees that filtered out the hot sun. When the slips were transplanted in long narrow troughs of rich soil and their vines intermingled, they would look like beds of morning glories. She would be paid in sweet potatoes.

At the foot of the mountain in a sandy loam, Father planted the sweet potatoes. Higher up he put a short row of broom corn. Above these were pole beans which, when they climbed to the tops of the poles, would look like rows of green tepees circling the mountain. At the top was the cornfield, so evenly planted that the symmetry of it changed with each footstep. We had always had a big garden but nothing like this vast field Father had laid out this year.

My brothers, coming home after a day's work there, sore-muscled and sunburned, had harrowing tales to tell of narrow escapes from copperheads and rattlesnakes that inhabited these wild, rocky mountains.

Father worked diligently to overcome what he called a "lazy streak" in us. He gave orders like an army sergeant, which he had been, and once given, we weren't allowed a moment's hesitation in carrying them out, and with no "back talk." That was the rule that choked me. "I'm not going to harangue with a bunch of children all day," he'd tell Mother.

His presence was like a high spiked fence, shutting out everything but what he chose to admit. Mother lightly called it "ruling with an iron hand." We could argue our way out of anything with her. When Father wasn't home, the house was full of arguing and even fighting and hair pulling. Mother paid no attention. But the creaking rusty hinges of the big front gate alerted everyone.

One day, a little after daylight, still wearing a long cotton nightgown and wrapped in one of Mother's tattered housecoats, I took my breakfast—a hot biscuit, flat and heavy because there was no baking powder in it, soaked in molasses—to one of the big swings on the front porch. For the thousandth time, I stared at the little streams and gullies that lay hidden by day in deep green entanglements on all the mountainsides, but were at this hour softly defined by rising mist. The mountain writhed as the mist rose, moved, changed shapes, then disintegrated into wispy trails that disappeared into cool clean air. In the distance over the river, was a valley of fog, rolling and turning as the sun burned it full of holes.

Father opened the screen door and stepped out on the porch, pulling a poke of Bull Durham tobacco from his shirtpocket. Sitting on the top step of the porch and with great care lest he drop a speck of tobacco, he rolled a cigarette from the limp, half-filled cloth bag. Putting the end of the yellow twine drawstring between his teeth, he closed it tight.

"The boys are workin' the garden today, the taters are full of bugs. I guess you're goin' to have to help me hoe corn."

"Hoe corn?"

"Hoe corn."

Had Father lost his mind? Leaving the swing, I ran through the house to find Mother in the kitchen. "Father says I have to hoe corn today. I'm not a fieldhand, Mother. I'd rather starve."

"You've no choice. They's a hat on that nail." She pointed to the back of the kitchen door.

I took my time getting dressed, my thoughts in furious turmoil. When is Father going to learn that I'm grown up—that I can decide what I want to do and what I don't want to do? I'm fourteen years old and I don't want to hoe corn. Who's going to tell him that I'm no longer going to do everything that he says to do?

We climbed the mountain, not speaking a word. He carried two hoes and a bucket of water with a tin cup wired to the bail. I offered to carry nothing. Reaching the cornfield, we stood a minute to get our breath. I stared sullenly back down the hill. After putting the pail of water in the shade, he handed me a hoe and said that he'd take the second row, I could take the first, and that we'd start at opposite ends.

He set to work methodically and single-mindedly, moving through the cornfield with confidence and ease. The earth turned over in dark moist mounds at the touch of his hoe encircling the spiked green plumes . in a pattern so precise that every hill looked exactly like every other hill.

My hoe was heavy and dull. The weeds were tough and elusive, the earth dry and dusty. When the hoe didn't hit a rock and glance off in a flinty sound, it filled my shoes with dirt. The blades of corn cut my legs into scratches and, when I sat down to empty the dirt from my shoes, cut my face. Salty sweat made the scratches itch and sting.

Full of self-pity I listlessly hacked at the weeds and constantly wiped at the sweat streaked with tears. Full of rage, I attacked the weeds violently, cutting the hearts out of them. In contrast to Father's neat even rows, mine were ragged, careless and trodden. Fire from a burning sun began to fall on me. It beat down in vertical hot shimmers, blurring my vision so that I staggered along conscious of nothing save the exact spot where my feet stood. The world around me pressed suffocatingly close.

Suddenly, like a breeze from a cool, deep green holler, a sound swept over me. It swept the cornfield from my feet. It swept the sun from the sky. I stood, not breathing, to listen. The whole mountain had come alive with the sound of fingers moving up and down the strings of a guitar in chords like a wind that whirled everything from its path. The music was coming from one of the company houses on the ridge across the creek. Yesterday the house looked vacant and today it still looked empty—its windows were closed and its doors were shut, but a man playing a guitar was sitting on the steps of the porch.

His music was moving in headlong momentum, getting faster and faster. He began singing about a freight train, its brakes gone, heading downhill toward a dangerous curve. The engineer, the brakeman, and the flagman were all giving orders as the train and the music roared on. I recognized the voice and, dropping my hoe to the ground and folding my arms, stood listening.

The rhythm was suddenly broken by Father's angry voice. He had reached the end of a row and gone to the shade of a mulberry tree for a drink of water. He was calling me to come.

"That's Ab Bolyne!" I said, a little too ecstatically.

"Nobody but a fool would set and pick and sing in the middle of the day in a famine like this," he said contemptuously. "Don't you remember last winter when he stopped three times a week for supper?"

I remembered. He'd always had his guitar with him. He was a dark-haired handsome bachelor who had drifted into Letcher from nowhere. I had already made him into a medieval wandering minstrel—an ancient balladeer who deserved everyone's undivided attention. He could be the hero of a tale anyone would want to write. He lived in an unused shed attached to Jep Blair's barn where he fed the animals once a day for his rent. Beyond that his finances were unknown.

"Get yourself a drink and get your hoe," Father commanded. With not a breath of air moving, I trudged through the row of hot corn to find the hoe.

Ab had started a new song, one that had been created on the steps of the Letcher County Court House. In it the man sentenced to jail was the hero, his poor mother the martyr, and the sheriff was the villain. The sheriff would pay dearly for this arrest at the next election. I knew all the people that Ab was singing about, and I cheered him on. My hoe was lighter. The long rows were shorter. The weeds were soft and yielding as I sped along on the wings of Ab's song.

Father passed me in the middle of the row, muttering, ". . . hard to believe . . . workin' like a dog . . . Ab pickin' and singin' . . . winter comin'." The music had angered him, or not exactly the music but my attention to it. He had hoed two rows to my one. "I may leave you the last ten rows and you may be here listening to Ab till dark."

"How can you expect Ab to dig and scrape in the dirt, Father, when he owns no land? Does that make him bad?"

"Not bad. Shiftless. And you follow right along with him." He turned his back and sank his hoe deep into the ground.

Ab's fingers were moving across the strings in a mighty crescendo. His voice had authority as he began singing about God giving Noah specific instructions on how to build an ark "out of gopher wood without the bark." The music slowed, his tone changed to pleading, pleading for the people to take heed and come into the ark to be saved. The guitar beat a steady staccato as the rain began to fall. It beat on into vengeance, vengeance on a world of unbelievers.

Father was a little way up the hill from me. Leaning on the hoe, I called, "I'm not sure that's Ab, Father. It sounds like the Rain God calling for Thunder and Lightning to tear the Sun from the sky."

I smiled. I'd just read something like this in an Indian tale.

"Tear the sun from the sky?" He shook his fist toward the man on the porch, glared at me, threw his hoe down and stalked off to the mulberry tree.

"You can't shut out Ab's music with your spiked fence, Father, nor this fiery sun from the sky," I said, but not out loud.

I followed him and we sat down on the ground. The sun moved the shade to the edge of the corn. I leaned down and wiped the sweat from my face with the hem of my dusty dress. When Father took off his hat, his hair was wringing wet. His collar was soaked, his eyes were flaming, and he was boiling inside. He handed me a cup of water and shook his calloused finger in my face. "Let me remind you when you were learning to read, you read me a story over and over about a grasshopper that danced and sang across the meadow all summer long." He paused, pointed toward the porch. "He starved to death in a frozen winter."

The music was silenced. Ab was gone. I burst into tears.

"Drink yo' water," he commanded.

"I don't want any water, Father. I hate this cornfield. I hate hoein' corn. I don't ever want to set foot in this place again," I shouted, sobbing louder than ever.

He moved closer and put his arm around my shoulders. "Some people'er not cut out for cornfields." He patted my shoulder. "Let's go home now. This sun's too hot."

THAT MAN

The house was wedged tightly between two mountains, leaving only enough room on one side for a path connecting the front and back yards. On the other side, the house sat at the very edge of the creek, that in high water flowed under the house. From the back yard, one looked straight up into the face of a dismal cliff, shadowy in the day and pitch black at night. The front porch looked toward an open, flat place covered with enough knee-high grass to graze a cow and ending at the foot of another mountain. The creek that drained these three mountains flowed between steep overgrown banks that exposed huge rocks when the water was low. The creek had no name. No old settler had ever stayed there long enough to give it a name, and too few people went that way to call it anything.

When the house changed hands at the County Clerk's office, it had the necessary appurtenances to be called an "estate." Under a ledge in a rock above the kitchen door was a spring of fresh mountain water so cold that in summer the rock over it sweated in the heat of the day. Outside the gate was a cave which was braced up with railroad ties to hold a thin vein of coal. Slate, which had been gathered in the darkness of the cave, now lay in a dull gray heap at the cave's entrance.

For over a mile, the house was guarded by a blue clay road running parallel to the creek. Resembling a slimy, glistening serpent, its glassy surface was almost impossible to tread in even the lightest dewfalls. But any road on this side of the mountain would have been laid in slithery clay. The house was abandoned. The sinister stare of its black-reflecting windows compelled the passerby to stare back at them. At sundown the house crawled out of sight, merging with the dark shadows of the mountain.

Children in Letcher, sent to bring the cows home at milking time, were fearful that the cow might have wandered to the grassy place in front of the house. Hunters admitted they felt "quar" searching for prey there and avoided it altogether at night because of the treacherous terrain.

Joe Finley, looking for a lost hunting dog one day, came back to tell the men at the store, "I come down out o' the woods to cross the creek and standin' thar on the porch was a man. I te' ye, he's a walkin' cadaver, and it weren't no haint." He paused to let this sink in, then went on, "They's smoke in the chimney." That settled it; somebody was living there.

Indeed, he was tall and so pale he looked as if he'd just risen from his deathbed. Wherever he'd lived before, it was plain that he'd been indoors for months, and for all these people knew, he could have spent that time here at this abandoned house. His bony face had the contours of jutting rocks. His eyes were sunken pools, shadowed in the caves of their sockets. They had the look of utter hopelessness in them. His long gaunt figure would suddenly appear before me, on out-of-the-way paths, walking with a motion so easy it seemed to level the steep ground. Everybody had met him at some time in one place or another. They had smiled and said, "How ye do?" But he neither smiled nor answered, so they no longer greeted him. He told no one his name, and nobody asked. If necessary they would call him "Mister" to his face. Behind his back they referred to him only as "That Man."

Neighbors sitting on our porch agreed that he was a lone man. "Away from his own hearthstone is a man with the heart took out o' him," Green Honeycutt said. "When you see a man with that look of hopelessness in his face, they ain't nothin' to be done."

"If he wants to be let alone, we'll let him alone," Father said.

One evening, two men were playing checkers in Lige Banks' store. One of them was J.M. Caudell, the only fat man in Letcher and its champion checkers player. His opponent was Custer Mullens, who had two gold teeth, which gave his smile a special brightness. Custer was second in checkers only to J.M. Jim-Tom Bailey, who had been married just about two months and had stopped by to get his wife a can of Pet Milk for her morning coffee, was watching the game intently. Lige was straightening out the shelves, his normal chore at the end of each day, when the screen door opened and That Man walked up to the counter.

The men glanced up, met no eyes, and wordlessly resumed their game.

"Do you'uns carry Red Ox twists?"

Lige nodded and got the tobacco for him. The gaunt customer paid him with a twenty-dollar bill, causing a slight flurry, as Lige had to empty the till and his pockets to make enough change. That Man walked out "unnoticed." Once he was out of earshot, J.M. said, "He's from Tennessee. He didn't say 'you all.' He said, 'you uns'."

"Yessir, and he's runnin' from the Law," Custer put in. "He walked in with his hands open and his palms turned out, empty. He's carryin' no far arms."

"Anybidy carryin' a twenty-dollar bill these days had sold somethin' mighty valuable," Lige said, suspicion in his voice.

"He's kilt somebidy and had to sell out and run," Jim-Tom contributed. "You reckon it was over a woman?"

"He's too old fer a hot-headed killin' like that, Jim-Tom." Custer's voice had instruction in it for the young man. J.M. adjusted the galluses of his overalls. "We've got a choice here, boys. We can turn him in, or we can talk it around and see what the other boys thank. If he's a feudin' it don't bother us nohow, and he ain't botherin' a soul."

Lige took his hands off the back of the chair he'd been leaning on and went to the back of the store to lock the door. "See you tomar', boys."

The men rose from their chairs and, putting the checkerboard on a shelf, left the store.

For months the subject of the stranger was predominant in all conversations. Groups of men, as was their habit, gathered Sunday afternoons to hunch on the ends of the railroad ties and talk about That Man, as they whittled and smoked. "As long as He give That Man a foothold here," Whitt McFadden insisted as he pointed skyward, "hit ain't up to us to prise him loose."

"Nosir, and him not a botherin' a soul," someone would always add.

Among themselves, the men kept trying to defend their actions in not turning That Man over to the Law. Father argued more persuasively for him. "That Man brought hisself to trial; he judged hisself and found hisself guilty. He sentenced hisself to spend the rest of his life hid out in the Godforsaken holler. Let's let him alone."

Perhaps Father defended him because of the evening when Kin, the plowman, held a singing on our porch and That Man walked by. Pausing, he listened with interest, then sat on our gate step with his head in his hands. At the end, he left without speaking to anybody. Now, Father's speech seemed to strike a note of compassion. When the men took a poll, they voted for leniency. "Nosir, he ain't botherin' a soul. Let's let him go unnoticed."

One night in the fall, following a frost that had blackened the seeds and left them limp and fallen, That Man walked down the creek and out of the holler for the last time. He turned right on the blue clay road and knocked on the first door he came to. It was opened by Homer Alcorn, who stepped out on the porch and closed the door behind him.

"I been sick awhile and I ain't goin' to make it this time." Holding out a handful of bills, he went on, "I'd be mighty obliged, Sir, if you'd see to it that I'm buried."

Homer made no attempt to take the money. He was overcome with pity for the cadaverous stranger who looked as though he could hardly stay on his feet.

"Anywhere's thar around the place'll do . . . above the creek aways." He pressed the money into Homer's hand.

"I'll see that you're buried, Mister. My word." He reached out and shook hands with the stranger.

Homer was a "worked out" miner who, with his wife Leuralee, tried to stay alive on a small veteran's pension. After the visitor left, he killed and dressed a chicken. After his wife cooked it and dropped dumplings into the broth, the pair walked at the edge of the bushes above the clay road, struggling to make their way to the old man's house with the hot steaming pot.

"Come in," he said at the sound of their knock. He lay on a bed with a corn shuck mattress that rustled like paper as he lifted his head and leaned on his elbow.

"I brought you a good supper, Mister," Leuralee greeted him. However, he didn't eat the food they brought or accept the medicine they offered. Leuralee left the pot of chicken on the cold stove and walked home alone with a deep sadness bursting her heart at the thought of his dying with no family to comfort him. "Let us hope he's found God," she said aloud.

Homer, left alone with the stranger, built a fire in the little grate to warm the room, then sat at the stranger's bedside until daylight. Through the long hours of the night, he couldn't tell if the old man was sleeping or was unconscious. Next morning, before going to bed, he walked to Green Honeycutt's store to ask him to locate a few men to take turns sitting with That Man. "Hit'll only be a day or two."

Several days later, in late October, J.M. and Homer sat at the old man's bed. The coal-oil lamp on the center table left the room in shadow, illuminating only the pale face on the pillow and the two men in their vigil. Seeing that death was hovering over the old man, J.M. shook him by the shoulder and inquired, "You want me to get Preacher Bennington, Mister?"

"No, no. My soul is too blackened to ever be cleansed," he gasped before lapsing back to sleep. The two men found this disconcerting. It was out of perspective: no tearful family, no doctor, no sad songs being sung, and no urgent prayers for his soul. "Who'd ever watched a man die in total silence?" they seemed to ask as they shook their heads.

Around midnight the old man roused himself, rising from his pillow into a half-sitting position. His eyes had new light in them, a light that was lit by the kindness of the people. "I don't aim to make no deathbed statemint," he asserted in a soft apologetic voice.

"We didn't come to hear no statemint," they answered. The stranger, without any further comment, settled back onto his pillow and lapsed into uneasy sleep. Towards daylight J.M. and Homer heard a deep sigh, then nothing more.

In early November the new moon found its way through the bare branches of a lone beech tree that stood above the creek, illuminating a solitary white tombstone on which no word was chiseled. At last the holler had an old settler, one who would be there forever, lying on a mountain with its back toward Tennessee. The moon put a silvery sheen on the little creek flowing over the whispering rocks, the murmuring sound mingling with the wind composed an eternal cantabile in a eulogy to That Man.

DRAGON'S TEETH

M iss Ashton had the face of a woman in a strong
wind. The skin swept back tight from taut cheekbones, and was pulled back even tighter by long hair
stretched to where it was pinned at the back of her head.
Tendrils of black hair escaping the pins floated backward
in wispy trails.

She was a widow with three grown sons. They lived
in a place off to itself, on a dusty road on the ridge that
ran along Crase's Branch. Roses climbed over the
gateposts and on up to lose themselves in the branches of
a sycamore tree that grew just beyond the fence. There
was an unfinished, homemade look about their house, like
the square ones that children draw with windows uneven
and the path to the door straight as a ruler. Its four rooms
were large and airy, but the generous hand of the builder
had stopped at the porches. Indeed, they were little more
than stoops with barely room for a swing and one chair.

The well-box at a back corner of the house was green,
matching the weeds that grew around it. Lying in front of
the well was a large flat stone to keep spilled water from
making mud. A shed leaned against the trunk of a pear
tree on the brink of a gully behind the house. It had no

door, and odds and ends not in use were thrown into it. Apple trees gone wild overflowed the gully with shade in summer. A clothesline was strung from the back yard to the front. On wash day it sagged under the weight of wet denim overalls which had been washed on a board and wrung by hand. Water dripping from them fell to the grass, which was greener here than in the rest of the yard.

Miss Ashton took in a little money quilting for people. She charged a dollar per spool of thread used for piecing and quilting in her fine hand stitching. It usually took about two spools of thread to make a quilt. The large quilting frame hung from hooks on the ceiling and was drawn up out of the way in the evening. Hour in and hour out, day in and day out, she sat at the frame pushing and pulling the needle through the soft cotton. Her arm came up at regular intervals in a flowing, ritualistic movement as she pulled the thread through the quilts. As she worked, she hummed sacred tunes mostly written by Isaac Watts or John Newton.

Her sons were unalike as three total strangers. Ulas, the oldest, was about twenty. Although he had a light frame, his hands were large and covered with downy hairs. In the overlay of his light hair, a few strands of brassy gold gave his whole head a soft gleam. His face was evenly featured with a sprinkling of freckles. His blue eyes saw the world through the pages of books. Still going to school, he would leave Letcher after the first hard frost and, carrying his clothes and books in a coffee sack, walk the eighteen miles to Caney College. Since no one else ever had any reason to go in that direction, Ulas had to make his own path over the mountain in order to shorten the trip. A lot of people said that he had a disordered mind "to study things that were neither here nor there." He could study all the concepts and theories that he chose, but the spontaneous response to the realities of the hills he lived among would hold him tight.

Corb, the second son, could have been a direct descendent of Chief Black Hawk, so dark was he. Shades of black played in his eyes like sunlight on a piece of coal. His hair, not often cut, was as black and shiny as the tail feathers of a crow. He wandered alone from hill to hill, digging ginseng, which he sold for thirty-five cents a pound to Dr. Isom down the river. Mostly he chose to spend his time outwitting and catching small animals and birds. He made traps of the things they were familiar with—grasses into nets, branches into gallows, and rocks into dead-falls. In the green shade of the paths he could be seen leaping uninhibited over logs and gullies with a smile that flashed as white as the tail of a deer.

Jun, the youngest, was a hunter of renown, with such strong kinship with dogs that the people marveled. At home he kept the dogs under the apple trees near the gully. Their large enclosures of chicken wire were widely separated so they wouldn't mingle their habits. Jun could sit on a log in the woods while Frisky, his rabbit dog, would bring the quarry straight to his master. He was the happiest hunting dog Jun had, and Jun would talk to him in laughing, foolish words as Frisky danced around his feet. But to Bonus, the fox hound, Jun would talk as solemnly as to a preacher. Bonus never wagged his tail nor danced around the feet of his master. Bonus was the master. When Jun walked into the enclosure to feed him, Bonus stood aloof, his regal head held high. Jun would drop down on one knee and whisper something in his ear. Bonus would then flex his muscles and in one long fluid movement he seemed to float to his eating dish.

Everybody in Letcher respected Bonus. Lying in their beds at night, they could hear his hoarse baying from one of those dark mountains, where Jun had unleashed him and then had built a fire in the cool mountain night as he waited for the telltale sound. He could tell by the hound's voice the minute he picked up the trail of a fox. Hound and fox would run miles and miles, but Bonus would slowly circle the exhausted fox back to where Jun waited. Jun's purebred dogs had been trained never to kill an animal. One clean shot from his rifle did that.

Not wanting to ruin a good hunting dog, and not being happy a minute without a companion, Jun acquired a mongrel named Streak. Never allowed in the woods, Streak moved in slow, heavy steps, following Jun from house to house when he made his calls selling rabbits, squirrels, and opossum ready for the pot. He sold his hides in Hazard. In early twilight almost any evening he sat on our porch, along with a few neighbors, telling tales of hunters long since gone.

Jun was built like a bulldog, short and thick and powerful. His strength was in his neck and shoulders. His smoky blue eyes belied the quickness with which that strength could be mustered. He liked people only a little less than he liked dogs, but he liked me best of all, or so he had written in a little note that he slyly passed to me at Green Honeycutt's store.

Of an evening on our porch he directed most of his conversation to Father, with a few warm glances at me when he thought no one was looking. I clearly read his glances, and when I had an errand to do for Mother I'd go out of my way to pass his house. He'd come to the gate and invite me in. We'd go to the back yard and sit on a log after I'd greeted each dog. "You know somethin'," he said one day, "you'd be scared to death up there in the mountains if I weren't with you." He reached over and took my hand. Then the screen door slammed. When Miss Ashton heard talking in the yard, she always came out. Once, joining us on the end of the log, she reflected, "I'll say one thang, the woman who gets Jun will never have to wash a dish. Them dogs'll lick everthang clean."

On winter nights Jun'd bring ears of popcorn which he'd hand to Mother as a little gift. We'd sit around the fire as he'd tell Father a new exploit of Bonus. "He took that fox clean over into the next county, two days 'fore he brought it in." Some nights I'd make molasses taffy, and it took two people to pull it back and forth till it had a pale yellow color. Then we'd sprinkle flour on the oil cloth-covered table and lay it in long ropes where it would be cut into brickle chunks called "pulled candy." Jun always volunteered to help pull it and our hands would touch.

As surely as Spring came, and as surely as the sap rose in the big trees, a primeval urge rose from the depths of Miss Ashton's soul to pay obeisance to the earth god. She had to plant something, anything, anywhere. And while the plants might lie unattended for the rest of the summer, the seeds were carefully embedded in the bosom of the Spring earth. She could no more resist this urge than she could fly.

One day in early Spring Miss Ashton left her quilting and went to the front porch. Corb was sitting on the top step, the blade of a knife flashing as he rounded off a prong for a slingshot. He heard the screen door open and shut, but he didn't look up. Lying in the porch swing, its rusty hinges clanking as he pushed himself to and fro with one foot, Ulas was committing to memory a Tennyson poem to prepare himself for the following semester at college. He was absorbed in the vision of another world as spoken by his namesake, Ulysses, so many centuries earlier:

> Yet all experience is an arch wherethrough
> Gleams that untraveled world whose margin fades
> Forever and forever when I move.
> How dull it is to pause, to make an end,
> To rust unburnished, not to shine in use!

And he felt a kinship with the ancient wanderer when he spoke of an unquenchable thirst for adventure and learning:

> And this gray spirit yearning in desire
> To follow knowledge like a sinking star,
> Beyond the utmost bound of human thought.

The slam of the door and the sudden appearance of his mother drew him into the present. But, like Corb, he didn't lift his eyes to acknowledge her.

"Where's Jun?" Miss Ashton asked.

"Feeding his dogs," Corb answered, still not looking up.

She turned to Ulas. "Go get him." She lifted the book from his hands and threw it on the chair.

Ulas returned with Jun. Coming around the house, they stooped under the clothesline and stood in the front yard.

Miss Ashton came down the steps to the yard and, facing the steps, demanded Corb's attention. "I want that lot over there plowed today." She pointed across the creek. "From that gum tree to that clump of locusts." Their eyes followed to where she was pointing. There was no dissent, so Miss Ashton went back to her quilting.

For no reason the boys could see, their mother always wanted something planted in rows, mostly Irish "taters," and they all knew that by Fall nothing could be found for the weeds. But to ignore her demands in the Spring meant they'd have to suffer her anger all summer.

It took about an hour to free the plow, harness, and lines from the year's debris under which they lay, but finally they dragged the plow from the shed and set out to cross the creek, walking in silence. On reaching the edge of the lot, Corb set down the heavy wing-tipped bottom plow, and Ulas attached it to the wooden shaft. Jun stood to one side watching as they gathered and tied the lines together, and then without a word he stepped forward and they hitched him into the traces. These were tied and came up over his head from the back and fastened to a board that fitted across his chest. Handholds were shaped at each end of a board where the lines fitted through notches. Jun groped for the ends of the board as Ulas picked up the traces.

I sat in the swing on the back porch and watched as every muscle in Jun's body tightened against solid bone when he leaned forward, and with a lurch of the plow, began to walk slowly across the field. As the plow moved, the earth began to turn, rolling over in a soft brown ridge that Corb walked on as he held the plow handles with both hands. Corb's voice rose and fell in soft "gees" and "haws," and like a mule Jun obeyed. When they hit a root or a stone and Corb hollered "whoa," Jun stopped and took a step backwards to wait for the plow to be freed. On like a mule, Jun plodded, back and forth, his head down, his shoulders taut, his body sweating in the hot sun as he followed Ulas who was leading him to keep the rows straight.

As the sun got hotter, I took them a bucket of cold water. After they sat to rest a minute, I went back to the porch and watched them continue their work. The plowed pattern changed very slowly into a long narrow rectangle, and Jun was covered with sweat and dirt. He didn't lift his head any more. Corb watched a bird on the wing as it dipped in a flash of sunlit color, his eyes following it on into the green hills far away. Ulas was pondering on Darius' marching army, trying to reconcile it with something historical he'd read in the Bible. Jun was straining with every muscle in his body against that hard rocky earth.

Suddenly, in the middle of an unfinished furrow, Jun stepped out of the traces and without a word hit Corb in the mouth, in the bony part just above the teeth. Corb's head jarred backwards as he dropped between the plow handles, spitting out a tooth and oozing blood from his mouth. Ulas ran over, raising a halting hand. Jun swung and hit him in the side of the head hard enough to turn him around. As he turned, Ulas' foot caught in the traces and he fell. Jun dragged him over close to Corb and began stomping them both. His heavy shoes came down hard, as the freshly plowed earth was dampening with the blood from Corb's mouth.

With the speed of a rattlesnake, Corb streaked up at Jun, hitting him under the chin so fast and so hard that Jun staggered backwards. The blow stunned him for a minute, long enough for Ulas to get up and hit him square in the jaw, then duck for Corb to strike him. They took turns hitting till Jun finally fell. I ran over there with a cloth dipped in water, accusing Corb and Ulas of trying to kill him, then wiping the blood from Jun's swollen, bruised face that was already turning blue. Ulas didn't answer. He was holding a loose tooth back up into its socket. Corb looked away. Jun sat up slowly and tried to pull himself to his feet by the plow handles. Ulas and Corb each put an arm around him and patiently lifted him upright.

A glassy sheet of sunshine lay over the stillness, drying the blood in the furrow to black. Corb shook the plow loose from the wooden shaft and picked it up to carry home. Ulas gathered the rawhide traces together, and I offered to carry Jun's load.

"You lost yo' head there for a minute, Jun." Ulas said, very softly.

"I shore did," Jun replied apologetically.

Miss Ashton, hearing the gate open, stuck her needle upright in the quilt and came to the front porch from where she called, "What's brangin' you all home this time o' hour?"

"Hit tore the hide right off us." Corb answered.

As the boys moved closer, she looked from face to face, surveying the ruin before her, and wailed, "Lord in His Heaven, Ruler of this earth, you boys been into it."

"We'll plant what we plowed tomar'." Ulas promised.

Streak plodded over to where Jun slumped against the sycamore tree, but was kindly pushed away. "Hold off, boy. They ain't enough hand left to bother lickin'." Jun's smile was swollen shut, but his eyes were friendly.

"Well, that parcel oughta grow dandy patch o' dragons if teeth'll spring," Ulas told his mother.

CINDY

White smoke rose above the frost-covered house tops into the early morning mist, leaving pools of black tarpaper showing around the warm chimney bases. Footprints in the lane were frozen into perfect patterns, making the ground uneven and difficult to walk on. Cindy, carrying an armful of fodder and an empty lard bucket, made her way over the frozen lumps toward the milk gap at the end of the lane. Guerney, her cow, was waiting with a heavy udder to be milked.

Cindy had no children. Her husband had been dead now for about five years, and on her way to milk she was suddenly overwhelmed by sentiment as she huddled in her husband's old army overcoat. Its tightly woven fibers of olive green wool were enough to rebuff the coldest frost. The eagle insignia on the brass buttons gave the coat an official precedence over every other garment in the house. And there was forever clinging to the coat a strong smell of tobacco, for in summer the trunk in which the coat was stored was lined with broad tobacco leaves to keep the moths away.

In the warmth of the old World War I overcoat, Cindy felt a closeness to her husband, remembering how often she'd buttoned it for him, and the hug and kiss that he'd give her for doing it as he stepped through the door. But this morning the coat imparted a sadness that had Cindy on the verge of tears, for yesterday Preacher Bennington had asked her to marry him. There was nothing romantic about his proposal. He'd simply pointed out very matter-of-factly, and rather successfully he hoped, that "A man around the place would be a great help."

Mother nodded in agreement as Cindy told her this.

"Hah!" Cindy contradicted. "I told him I didn't have time to wash and iron and cook for a man."

"Well, that's the truth." Mother agreed with this, too. "A man does take up a lot of a woman's time waitin' on him hand and foot."

Cindy was over sixty years old. Her hair, still mostly brown, was coiled on top of her head in a loose circular bun in the shape of a donut. It looked for all the world like a bird's nest with the little wispy strands escaping all around it. Below the bird's nest, over her forehead, she wore a white cloth "headache band." It was tightly wrapped and tied in the back. She said it warded off headaches and kept the hair out of her eyes.

Cindy's house, which was built in an L shape, sat below the other houses on the hillside, just above the creek. Whether frosty or dew-sprinkled, its roof was the first to catch the morning sun coming over the mountain. Flat stones connected it to the front gate, creating one of the few walks in Letcher.

There were cherry trees in the front yard, and to keep the neighborhood children from breaking the branches by climbing to get the fruit, Cindy had placed two bee gums amongst the trees. When she herself picked the cherries, she shared them generously with all the children who lived nearby. When she put on her "apparatus" to "rob the bees," she gave the children chunks of comb honey, which they ate with drippy, sticky fingers later licked clean.

Cindy was a "Doctor Woman" who also occasionally delivered babies when Becky Browning was on another case. Although Cindy was competent and well-liked, Becky was preferred because she prayed a lot and attributed her success to the Lord.

It was in the dead of night when I came awake as Mother shook me by the shoulder. She whispered to me to come to the kitchen where she had a fire in the stove. Our two year old, wrapped in a blanket in her arms, was coughing and struggling to breathe.

"The baby's sick. You've got to get Cindy," she said, handing me a coat from a nail behind the stove and then handing me the baby as she went through the house to turn on the front porch light.

Cindy lived down the hill and across the little creek that came down the mountain and flowed into Crase's Branch. The twenty-watt bulb from our porch barely lit my way as I stumbled along under the starlight and struggled to make out the shape of her house. More than seventy-five unseen houses were scattered in the dark landscape, invisibly mapped by barking dogs which slept under each of their front porches—brief and subdued barks, nothing like the frantic yelping that a passing animal would have drawn. Guerney, sleeping on a pile of straw, hove to her feet in heavy breathing as I nearly stumbled over her in the lane.

Cindy answered the door immediately, and I told her that the baby had the croup and that Mother wanted her to come. She went to the kitchen to put a few things in her little black leather grip. Roots, twigs and barks, which had been previously crumbled, shredded, pounded, then mixed, in required assortments, hung in back of the stove. The old pine dish-safe in the corner held everything but dishes: green Mason canning jars filled with sassafras, catnip, pennyroyal, and dozens of other things for teas and poultices. Ginger, also for tea, was kept in its store-bought box. The writing on the can stood out officially against the jelly jar full of dried linings of chicken gizzards used to stop vomiting. Sulphur, lard, molasses and honey were there in large quantities, stored in crocks, buckets, and jugs. On the wide ledge of a window sill lay an ancient worn volume of remedies.

Snapping her bag shut, Cindy put on the old army overcoat that fell almost to her knees. I followed her to the kitchen door where the two of us stepped out into the frosty night. We followed the faint gleam of our porch light and were soon greeted by Mother's look of impending doom.

"He can't hardly get a breath, Cindy. I'm worried to death."

"Now I'd be worried, too, if I ever knowed a young'n dyin' o' croup." She sat her bag on the table and, throwing off her coat, asked Mother to get her a skillet. She took three big onions from her bag, sliced them into the skillet, and, from a little brown paper poke, sprinkled brown sugar over them as she added two dippers of water. Then throwing a lump of coal into the stove and taking the poking stick, she stirred the fire into blazes. She boiled down the mixture until she could drain off about a cupful of brown syrup.

While the mixture cooled, she wrapped the onions in a piece of flannel to form a poultice which she then put under the baby's shirt next to his chest. The onions filled the kitchen with a mentholated aroma. Cindy gave the baby two teaspoonsful of the warm syrup. As he tried to swallow it he let out a gaspy croupy cough, spilling most of it. She gave him more.

We sat around the stove, the baby dozing fitfully, then coughing and crying. Mother and Cindy conversed in low, whispered voices, for it wouldn't do to wake the whole household and have children crying on every hand. Father at this time was working nights in the mines, and it would be a few hours yet till he'd be home at daylight. As the fire burned lower, we huddled closer to the stove.

After about an hour, Cindy gave the baby two more teaspoons of syrup. "Now, Laura, you take the baby and go to bed and sleep. He'll be all right." The baby had dozed off again.

"My thanks, Cindy, till you can be better paid," said Mother as she took her by the hand.

"Money wouldn't 'ave got me out on this cold night, Laura." She hugged Mother.

"Show Cindy to the gate," Mother whispered to me.

"I can find the gate. Don't you get out in this cold night, honey." Cindy patted my arm and trudged off into the cold darkness, the heavy overcoat flapping around her shoe tops, a dozen dogs announcing her exit.

There was another side to the "Doctor Woman," the side which drew me to her in fascination. Cindy was an artist. She wore aprons seven days a week, the prettiest on Sunday. These aprons were made of cotton feedsacks boiled in lye water and hung in the sun to bleach. She made some aprons of sugar sacks, the hundred pound size, which were more finely woven and somewhat thinner than the feedsacks. They, too, were boiled in lye water to get out the red and blue lettering.

There was no mistaking the flowers, copied from her garden or the wild flowers from the woods. They appeared as appliqued calico scraps or fine embroidery stitches. Hollyhocks had green pointed sepals coming up to cup the various shades of pink petals atop willowy stems. Her dark vibrant dahlias were folded and pleated like living flowers. Cosmos were her favorite. Their big open faces were simple enough for a child to cut out, but when Cindy worked little piles of French knots in their centers, making them look like a heap of tiny seeds sprinkled from a can, they took on a professional artistry. Leaves and stems were made of yellow, brown, or any other color that struck her fancy. Before they were ever sewed to the aprons, the pockets were stretched on embroidery hoops. Then buttercups, violets, and other tiny things from the woods were intertwined with vines and leaves and embroidered on the aprons in a glossy satin stitch.

A completed apron had no kinship to a sugar sack. If it had been framed and hung on a wall, it wouldn't have been out of place. Before the Sunday church service, it was not unusual for a knot of weary women to lift Cindy's apron by the hem, wondering how she made such beautiful pictures with cloth and thread.

Preacher Bennington, walking past them toward the church door, might as well have been invisible, since all

eyes were concentrated on the intricate beauty of these
aprons. Noticing this, he made a mental note to "rebuke"
them from the pulpit.

Cindy made a quilt each winter when she had more
time indoors. She said she designed them "out of my
head." That winter she'd made one that meandered all
over the bed in a labyrinth geometry that always led back
to the center. "I named it 'Prisoners Cell'" she said, pointing to the middle block. "It shows they's no escapin'."
She smiled, adding, "I wouldn't take a house and a farm
for it."

Each day we bought a gallon of buttermilk fresh out
of the churn from Cindy, and just before supper I was
always sent to get it in a tin lard bucket with a tight lid on
it. By the time I got home with it, the wire bail had my
palms burning like they'd been cut in two, even though I
kept shifting the heavy bucket from one hand to the other.
I endured this agony without complaint because I savored
the chance to look at the beautiful handwork and because,
to send me on my way, Mother always called out,
"Where's the milkmaid?" I knew from rhymes and fairy
tales that milkmaids were all beautiful and that it was not
unheard of for a Prince to marry a milkmaid. I didn't question how a Prince was going to find me in Letcher, in
Cindy's lane, when the highest official in this entire kingdom was a postmaster.

One day Cindy's face was set in an unfriendly pattern
when she opened the kitchen door and I handed her the
empty bucket. Preacher Bennington was sitting at the
table, and Cindy pulled out a chair for me while she filled
the pail.

"I was just telling Sister Cindy here that on Sundays she draws more interest from the woman with her aprons than I do with the Word." He gave a foxy little laugh to make what he'd just said not sound like a rebuke. Cindy and the preacher ignored each other during this speech. Then with his eyes still on mine, he added, "I'll tell you, young lady, the material things that people wrap theirselves up in, in this world, are as ashes on Judgment Day."

Cindy whirled around to the table and, looking me in the face, said, "And I'll tell you somethin', young lady, if you get yo'self all tied up in hellfire and damnation, day in and day out, you won't be fittin' to face no Judgment Day."

"Forgive me, Sister Cindy," he interjected as he raised a hand. "I was just trying to point out to this child here that if she reads the Word she'll see that pride and vanity in frills will never open the Gates of Heaven."

"Brother Bennington, when I'm making them aprons I'm as nigh to Heaven as I ever want to be," Cindy said, slamming the lid on the milk bucket.

He clucked his tongue, "Ah! The Devil puts strange words in our mouths."

Cindy opened the door for me, and I went out. She opened it wider and waited. Preacher Bennington finally picked up his Bible. As he went through the door, Cindy offered her hand and he took it, but neither spoke a word.

When I told Mother all this, she exclaimed, "Lord in Heaven! Does he want Cindy to wear an apron to church with 100% PURE CANE SUGAR wrote across her bosom?"

A few weeks later, Preacher Bennington came down with "the Fever," an illness that came on with the chills, and Cindy was asked to go look at him. She gave him a cup of hot ginger tea and put five quilts over him to sweat the fever out. She sat at the bedside all night after he was drenched with sweat, taking off one quilt at a time at long intervals until only two were left. Never having heard of a thermometer, Cindy kept testing his temperature by laying her hand on his forehead. At last he felt cool.

She stopped in at our house on her way home, to tell Mother he was better. "I'm going to make him some hot buttermilk biscuits and take him a jar of honey to go with them, the poor man," she added. Mother looked at Father, who was eating breakfast, but also studied Cindy's face as she stepped through the door, saying, "Guerney's waitin' for me at the milk gap."

As in Chaucer's poem, "the sweet showers of April had pierced to the root the drought of March," turning the lanes and paths of Letcher into muddy, slippery roads. April had passed into May when one sunny day Mother called through the window for me to come into the house. She was sitting on the edge of a bed in the children's room as I entered and stood before her. She took my hands in hers. "My time has come now. Take the children to Miss Mullen's house and go get Cindy." She held on to my hands, adding, "If anything happens to me, you take care of the children till they're old enough to take care of theirselfs."

I left the room choking and tearful at the thought of anything happening to Mother. Not knowing at the time that she would eventually have thirteen children. (And at this writing they are all alive.)

I returned home minutes before Cindy came bustling in. Her headband was startling white, and her undecorated apron was even whiter than the others. This meant that she was "on medical duty." She carried her little black bag. "Hits might nigh over now." she greeted Mother in a soft, warm, assuring voice, and sent me to the backyard to get an axe. When I returned, she carefully lifted her clean apron and, kneeling, stuck the axe blade downward in a crack under Mother's bed.

"Hit does no harm and hits been said for a hundred years that hit cuts the pains."

Mother trusted the axe, too.

Cindy went to the teakettle Mother had left on the stove. Filling a teacup with boiling water, she stirred a half teaspoon of black pepper into it and brought it to Mother. "This'll help open the womb." Turning to me, she said, "You go now and stay with the children. This'll be over in no time. I'll come and get you."

It seemed forever, but it was only about two hours later that Cindy came for us. Through it all, Father was sound asleep in another room, and she left it that way because he'd worked all night. I found Mother sitting in bed with a pile of pillows at her back. She was bright and smiling, having had no medications or anesthetic save Cindy's tea. She held the baby in the crook of her arm as we all filed past and kissed the top of his little hairless head.

But Cindy's delivery hadn't ended there. That evening she brought a big kettle of chicken and hot biscuits, and ate supper with us after taking Mother a plateful.

Because Cindy wore wire-rimmed spectacles, the people said, "You can trust her 'cause she can read." But

Father knew a man who carried spectacles around in his shirt pocket without knowing one word from another. With the Doctor Woman, however, it was not pretence. She could read. Her thumbed and worn volume of *American Remedies* attested to that. And those remedies benefited us on many occasions.

She daubed soot from the fireplace on deep cuts to staunch the bleeding. I had a black mark like a tattoo on my foot for years from the soot. "That's better'n bleedin' to death," Mother had said. Cindy wrung out cloths in hot water and turpentine, then spread them on the abdomen to cure a malfunctioning bladder. A bitter of wild cherry bark was given to women suffering middle-age maladies. Warm catnip tea was given to babies with colic, and a brew of slippery elm bark cured the "seven-year itch."

I became addicted to Cindy's cure for upset stomach: a glass of blackberry juice. Holding my stomach, I'd tell Mother that I needed some of Cindy's medicine "to settle it." She'd open a big green glass canning jar of berries and strain off a glass of liquid. I was convinced that its magical powers would cure anything it was prescribed for.

Cindy used the membrane from the inside of an egg shell to plaster over boils and "risin's" to bring them to a head. If the boils persisted, she gave a dose of sulphur and molasses taken internally "to clear the blood." She used poultices of hot cooked cornmeal to cure whitlows around the nails of fingers and toes.

Cindy never said these treatments would cure. She only said, "Hit'll do no harm." As for curing warts with the sweat from an axe blade, she said, "I'm not foolin' around trying to get sweat from no piece of steel."

Occasionally something came along that Cindy couldn't treat, and then she'd recommend a "specialist." Women who couldn't describe their aches and pains well enough for Cindy to put a finger on were sent to Brother Ely, the faith healer, who lived down the road about four miles in a little house so close to the railroad track that it seemed as if the whoosh of a roaring train would sweep the house into the Kentucky River.

Such was the case of Opal Saylers, who asked me to walk to Brother Ely's with her. She could have been called beautiful, except her face was drawn with tension and her eyes filled with worry. We walked that whole distance without saying more than a few words. It was like walking with a ghost woman.

Brother Ely was a tall, elderly black man who had noticeably long-fingered beautiful hands. Inviting us to sit at the hearth of his coal grate, he asked Opal a few questions.

"Some days I can't hardly get one foot 'fore the other'n," she told him. "And I get a headache the minute I open my eyes most mornin's, so bad I can't get my husband's breakfast."

"You can't get the children's breakfast either?" he asked cautiously.

Opal dropped her head and tearfully told him that she had no children. He stood up and asked her to stand. Laying one hand on her shoulder, he raised the other heavenward. "Lord, You've designed for this woman to walk alone with her husband. And I ask in Your Holy Name that You give her strength of body and peace of mind to follow the path You have put her on. In Your Name, we pray. Amen."

Clinging to him, Opal burst into tears. Attempting to comfort her, he said, "The Lord will walk with you from here on, Sister."

We were halfway home before she spoke. "If He walks with me . . . ," but couldn't finish her anguished thought.

The next Sunday, Brother Bennington strode to the pulpit and immediately called for a prayer "for those in our congregation who have strayed off into witchcraft." The people looked at each other in shock and bowed their heads. All except Cindy, who held her head high and looked at Opal.

"Who in God's earth was he talkin' about?" Mother asked when we got home.

"If he'd a wanted us to know, he'd a had guts enough to say," Father replied.

Cindy followed up on Opal's case by taking her a tin bucket planted with young geranium slips, telling her to keep it in a south window and well watered. If she did, she would have blossoms by Easter. "She needs somethin' to grow and nourish," Cindy confided to Mother.

Cindy sent me to a "specialist" too. I had crawled through a hundred-year-old rail fence and my face had come in contact with a nest of yellow jackets. Although only three of them stung me, my face was swollen grotesquely. I ran straight to Cindy, who commanded, "You go to Joe Brownin' directly. He chews tobacco and only a drenchin' of ambierre will take out that venom." With my head burning like fire, I ran to Joe's. Sitting on his porch, he saw me coming with my head in my hands and met me in the road. Standing in the middle, he spat a palmful of Brown Mule tobacco juice and smeared it over my face, away from my eyes. He blew on my face to dry the concoction, then put another layer of the thick amber juice over it. Uncle Joe stepped back a few feet and studied my face to see if he'd left a spot unsmeared.

"Wuz it waspers or yaller jackets?"

"Yaller jackets."

"You better not tangle with them fellers agin."

I staggered home and dropped into the swing. Cindy came and wrung out a towel in the icy water from the well and put it on my head, making it all feel better. It seemed she had become one of the family. Cindy was a child psychologist long before the term was generally known. "If he ain't done too much, a little peach switch'll do, but if you don't aim for him to do it agin, hickory'll hold up twice as long," Cindy told Mother, who followed this advice with only a slight change. Her strategy was to tell us she wanted a hickory switch or, on occasion, a peach switch, then send us to get our own. We'd go in dread, searching so long for one that would fit our misdemeanor that half the time Mother'd get busy doing something and say, "Lay it on the table till I get through here." And sooner or later, so that she would not be reminded of her task, the switch would disappear.

In other instances, Cindy could sound Biblical in her remedies for wrongdoing: "If a child blames something on another'n that gets switched and hit's found out, then he should get two whippin's, one fer the young'n that got switched and the rightful one comin' to him." Of course, these prescriptions were given in our hearing, which would provoke Mother to say, "Now you know what's comin'."

Few problems failed to yield to Cindy's psychological or physical remedies. In the case of J.J., however, all of her considerable skills were called on to solve his problem.

J.J., the newest baby in the family, was eleven months old. What hair he had was a soft yellow, so pale it looked almost white. His eyes were blue, diluted with a soft gray, and showed an alertness and curiosity in everything around him. His disposition was sunny and co-operative all day long, and he never seemed to tire. This made him one of the most beautiful and beloved babies we'd ever had.

However, things changed when Mother decided to wean him. At eleven months, he was the same age as the other children had been. Like them, he had learned to drink from the dipper and had eaten mashed potatoes and oatmeal from a spoon, in addition to gnawing on a chicken bone when he began teething. Learning to walk made him leaner, and as he toddled unsteadily across the floor he seemed taller. We talked to him in baby talk: "Go beddy? Go bye-bye? Wa-Wa?" (a drink). He only said three words, "No," "Ma Ma," and "Da Da." He nodded his head for yes.

For the first time, Mother hadn't nursed him that morning, and while the cereal cooked he cried "Ma Ma" incessantly. I put him in the high chair and offered him a bite of oatmeal thinned with milk and sweetened with a pinch of brown sugar. Shutting his eyes tight, he hid from me by putting both chubby hands over his face.

"J.J., where are you?" I called.

He peeked through his fingers, saw the spoon and knocked it from my hand. "No! No! No!" he cried.

I leaned down to retrieve the spoon from the floor and he swept the dish from the tray in one angry swipe. I spoke soothingly, urging him to eat as I put another spoonful close to his mouth. He turned his face away, holding his lips tightly shut. Mother said, "Put him down. When he gets hungry enough, he'll eat."

The minute I put him down he crawled to Mother and, hanging on to the hem of her dress, cried "Ma Ma" in a pleading tone. Mother unfastened his hands, took him by the shoulders, and turned him away. He flung himself back toward her, wrapping his arms so tight around her knee that she couldn't move. She loosened his arms and told me to take him outdoors.

At noon I again put him in the high chair and offered him baked sweet potato mashed with milk. "Umm, good," I told him. But even soothing words now made him angry. "No! No!" he screamed, striking at my face with both hands. I refused to believe that such indomitable will power could be centered in a child so young. I put the dish away and got a piece of bread. Putting it right against his lips, I pushed lightly to force it into his mouth. He opened his mouth and came down so hard on my finger with his sharp baby teeth that it drew blood. I had to slap his cheek to get him to open his mouth and cry so I could remove my finger. He was behaving like an animal caught in a trap, snarling and biting the hand that tries to free it. He sat there crying, his face hot and red.

My nerves were frazzled, he hadn't eaten or taken a drink all day. I left the kitchen and went to confront Mother. "Are you going to starve him to death in front of all our eyes?"

"Milady, watch your words. If you'd kept him out o' sight of me as you were told to do, he'd be eatin' by now." She only called me "Milady" when she was angry.

"You don't know him, Mother. He's never goin' to eat," I said tearfully, then marched back to the kitchen. There J.J. was still crying loudly, "Ma Ma, Ma Ma" with every breath he drew. I raised my voice even louder as I took him from the chair: "Are you going to be a mommy's boy all your life?" His hand streaked up, hitting at my face. "No, no."

Mother came to the kitchen. "I've sent to get Cindy. She may know what to do." Her voice sounded tired and defeated. I took J.J. to the front porch and laid him on a folded quilt in the swing to rock him to sleep. He, too, was exhausted. Cindy came on the porch steps, a big straw hat perched on her bird's nest of hair and with the headache band gleaming across her forehead. She hadn't brought the black bag this time. We all went through the house to the back porch so as not to wake J.J., and Mother explained the situation.

"We'll have this straightened out 'fore nightfall," Cindy said confidently. "With a child, Laura, you've got to let him make the choice of not nursin'. When you jist pushed him away and said 'No,' hit unsettled him." Cindy was older than Mother and talked to her "like a daughter." She added, "If you'd a called me first off, I'd a told you how to wean a child with no trouble."

"Well . . . I didn't know . . . ," Mother fumbled, her words like a little girl's being scolded. Cindy laid out her "cure," so Mother put a smearing of lard on her breast, then daubed soot from the fireplace over it. When this was completed, she pulled the bodice of her dress to cover it.

It wasn't long till we heard J.J.'s cry, "Ma Ma, Ma Ma." At this signal we all went back to the front porch where Mother picked him up and hugged and kissed him, finally sitting down with him in her lap. Before long he indicated that he wanted to nurse, so Mother pulled her bodice aside.

His eyes grew large as he stared at the black, unpalatable thing before him. He kept looking at it as though he were studying a difficult problem. Then closing his eyes tightly so that he could see the breast no longer, he began to nurse. Mother looked beaten.

"Well, this happens once in a while, but we ain't through yet," Cindy assured her. She revealed the rest of the "cure," which had to be postponed for at least two hours when J.J. would want to nurse again. Cindy was invited to supper so she could observe the results of her advanced remedy. While she and Mother cooked and chatted, J.J. played happily, his face lighted in smiles.

I took him a boiled potato mashed in milk and sat on the outside steps as I fed it to him. But soon he began crying, "Ma Ma, Ma Ma." Getting up, he wandered through the house looking for her, having no way of knowing what lay in wait. Cindy's new cure consisted of a fingertip of lard to hold three grains of black pepper on the breast.

When J.J. found Mother, he dropped to all fours, since he could crawl faster than he could walk. Reaching her, he pulled himself up by the hem of her dress and stood with both hands uplifted, waiting to be taken. She picked him up and put him in her lap.

She gave him the breast. He took it eagerly but immediately drew back, spitting, then sticking out his tongue so he could wipe it with his fingers. Mother offered to nurse him again but he had clearly had enough.

"No!" he said. Rubbing his lips, he climbed down from her lap.

The months passed, the seasons changed, but there was always a need for the wisdom Cindy could provide. It was to her that Mother turned when she found out that my three youngest brothers were committing a serious offense. On a hillside running about fifty feet above the road, they had collected six piles of rocks. Hiding behind some paw-paw bushes, each with a pile of stones, they showered rocks in front and behind any passerby on the road. Running from bush to bush, they followed the people till it became intolerable. Sam Hughes was annoyed enough to climb the hill without being seen and, once he was higher than the boys, clearly saw the source of this commotion. He came and told Mother.

She was distraught, embarrassed, and angry at the same time. "What will their father say?" she asked, wringing her hands. Turning to me, she said, "Go get Cindy as quick as you can."

As always, Cindy arrived quickly and, after hearing the story of the miscreants, assured Mother that help was at hand. "Now, Laura, you've gone all to pieces here over nothin'. I've parted many a boy from rock throwin' with the help of an old man I brought to life from Split Rock." The mountain she referred to could be seen in the distance from our house. Its whole top was solid rock split right down the middle, making a dark chasm that was full of rattlesnakes.

As Cindy explained her plan, Mother's handwringing stopped and she smiled in agreement. "Now, no matter what I say tonight, you uphold the boys," Cindy insisted.

Later, after the two youngest were put to bed earlier than usual, Mother gathered the rest of us in the middle room at dusk. Suddenly, the gate opened with a wild swing and then slammed shut. Slow, ponderous footsteps dragged up the steps and across the porch, accompanied by a clanking metallic sound.

"Shh," cautioned Mother as she put her fingers to her lips and listened to the loud pounding on the door. With much hesitation she opened it, but just barely.

There, in the rim of lamplight, stood a creature wrapped in an old motheaten buffalo robe. His feet were bound in coffee sacks tied on with twine, and his black hat, pulled low, met heavy black brows. Blood red streaks ran from the corners of his mouth and down his neck and red oozed from between fingers holding a heavy iron chain. Mother didn't have to invite him in.

He bowed low in the doorway. "I'm Bloody Bones. I live in Split Rock." He began laughing and ho-hoing like Santa Claus. "I hear you got boys around here that throws rocks at ever'bidy passin'. I love mean boys, my cave's full of 'em. Can I have 'em?" He slapped his knee and rattled the big iron chain.

"You've got the wrong house, Bloody Bones. I've got no mean boys here." Once Mother got into the act, she saw Cindy's drift. "I don't call boys bad when tomar' they're going to tell all them people that they won't throw any more rocks." Mother looked at the three who'd gathered around my chair and waited for their answer. They nodded in unison.

Bloody Bones took on a disappointed look. "Well, well, I don't take good boys." He turned and dragged his heavy chain down the steps. Mother, returning from closing the door and latching the gate where she and Cindy had congratulated themselves, shook her head, "For the life of me, what brought Bloody Bones to this house I'll never know. My children try to be good." The message was not wasted on the three boys who slept in the same big bed and whispered a long time before they fell asleep.

Cindy came over the next day to check on the effectiveness of the previous night's "cure" and to show a present she had received. Traces of pokeberry juice could still be seen between her fingers as she opened a little brown paper poke, the size a dime's worth of brown sugar would come in.

"Laura, look at what Brother Bennington brought me." Her face was alight with smiles as she put the poke in Mother's hands. I went over to peer in the little bag with Mother. It was full of all colors of embroidery floss.

"What on earth does this mean, Cindy?"

"Hit means I'll make him an embroidered mantelpiece like he ain't seen before."

LEAVING HOME

In Letcher County, Carbon Glow, Dixie Diamond and Blackey Coal Companies had hollowed the coal out of the mountains, and Franklin D. Roosevelt's NRA (National Recovery Act) could do nothing to replace it. People were laid off work, coal camps closed and no trains ran in Letcher. People who had no place to go lived in the empty camp houses.

One morning after breakfast Father remained at the table while he and Mother talked about hard times as she cleared the big kitchen table and wiped the oil cloth clean. She then brought him a penny pencil and rough tablet and he set to writing a letter to his sister Betty Deaton who lived on a farm near Wyoming, New York, between Buffalo and Rochester. Father told Aunt Betty how bad things were and that we had to get away from there or starve to death.

She wrote right back for us to come to New York State, that she had found an empty farmhouse we could rent very cheap near her, and that when we got there she would help Father find a job of some kind with the many farmers in the area. "Don't worry about how to get here, I'll send the boys with the truck to get you all. Just let me know when you can come."

As soon as Father sold our house, he wrote Aunt Betty that we were ready to come.

My oldest brother, James Willard, would not be coming with us. He had enlisted in the Army when he wasn't quite sixteen years old by getting an older man to verify that he was seventeen. He put in twenty years of military service mostly in the 82nd Airborne Division, starting just before World War II. He earned the Purple Heart and the Medal of Honor, and sent home an Army check regularly for years.

At ten o'clock one night about a week later, a big truck pulled up to our gate and Dick and George got out. Mother hugged and kissed them, Father shook hands and we children stood and stared at them. Next morning they put all the furniture, clothes and bedding that would fit in the truck, leaving room at the end for the children, Mother sat in front with the baby. A tarpaulin had been tied on so that it could make a roof if it rained or got cold at night. It was a long journey in a slow truck with no super highways and right down the middle of every city and village with a thousand red lights to stop for and a thirty-mile speed limit.

Three or four nights later, about eight o'clock, we drove into Aunt Betty's driveway. She hugged and kissed everyone and went to the kitchen where she cooked an enormous supper of pork chops, hot biscuits with cream gravy, mashed potatoes and applesauce. I couldn't sit up long enough to eat. I lay down on the sofa and fell asleep. For days I couldn't comb my hair, standing in the back of the truck in the wind had tangled it so.

Father found a job that he liked very much with a nearby farmer in an apple orchard. When winter came he worked with Dick and George in the woods, cutting down trees, sawing them into cord wood for delivery to a market in Buffalo. He loved working outdoors.

Here, in Wyoming, we revelled in the area's beauty, with Carleton Hill rising 1,612 feet above the broad, flat Oatka Valley. Studying it, Mother would say, "A few more feet and hit could have been a mountain." We were surrounded by friendly, generous farmers who went out of their way to welcome my parents and their children and to share with us their plenty. There were apple and peach orchards, meadows of beef and dairy cattle, fields heavy with corn, and acres of potatoes which were offered to us simply for the gleaning.

Yet there were wide cultural differences. The natives talked loudly. Mother said, "Hit's because of so much wind here, and they all work out in it." The houses were unfenced, giving the impression of pictures without frames, and with no admitting gates it seemed bold to walk right up to the door. Their front porches were narrow, nobody ever sat on them, and without hordes of children in the yards, the houses looked unpeopled.

As for the language, it was precisely spoken with g's and d's on word endings, and with a vocabulary peculiar to the region. The differences were so great that a storekeeper, having difficulty with Mother's Southern dialect, asked her what country she was from.

Mildly offended, she replied, "I'm an American."

It was the first blizzard, however, that determined the family's immediate future.

We had celebrated our first Christmas in the north, made joyful by a beautiful tree decorated with paper chains the children had made from the pages of an old catalog, and gifts for each child provided by the local church women. My gift, wrapped in real Christmas paper, was a small box of Coty face powder, the white and orange Art Deco box with the gold powder puff. The sight of it at a cosmetic counter, even now, brings brings back memories for me of that Christmas.

A few days later, gray clouds in the oval shapes of doves came pushing smoothly and silently over the summit of Carleton Hill. By noon they were dark charcoal, covering the sky from horizon to horizon and so heavy and low they seemed to barely skim the rooftops. They hung there in an eerie breathless silence. About four o'clock, a gust of wind came roaring across the top of the hill, pushing a solid wall of snow before it. Except it wasn't a gust; it was a steady blast that slammed into the side of the house with the roar and speed of a freight train. Carleton Hill, the Oatka Valley, the barn across the road, the whole world was obliterated in a deafening disorienting roar.

Father hadn't arrived home from delivering wood to Buffalo, and Mother was going from one whitewalled window to the other, wringing her hands as she stared at the reflection of her anguished face. Suddenly, the front door blew wide open with such force it scattered clothes and papers in every direction. The door between the living room and the kitchen slammed shut with an earsplitting crash. As the storm blew right into the house, Mother stood dead in her tracks, looking bewildered. The children began crying. Then we saw Father trying with all his might to shut the door behind him. We rushed to help till he got it locked. Half frozen in his skimpy clothes, he hugged the stove as close as he dared, to get warm.

Mother said she was "too tore up to cook," so we had a frugal meal of boiled potatoes with salt as the storm intensified. Raising her voice over the howling wind, Mother showed her exasperation. "Why on earth did you rent a house on top of a hill? They told you they had snowstorms here."

"Hit's just as bad down there," Father asserted, pointing toward the valley. Neither one of them used the word "blizzard" because they had never heard it.

When I took the children upstairs to bed, they saw the two or three inches of snow that had blown across the beds through cracks in the windows and refused to get into them. I took a load of quilts and pillows and made pallets along the wall downstairs, where they slept restlessly, turning and mumbling in their sleep.

The house bent and creaked with tearing sounds, and the room became as cold as if the stove weren't there. The electricity had gone off, leaving an old kerosene barn lantern with a black-streaked chimney as our only source of light. Father added wood to the stove, and we all stayed in the gloomy room that night with its murky shadows moving to the fluttery lantern wick and dimmed by puffs of smoke that occasionally seeped from every seam of the stove as the wind breathed down the pipes. The room and its people looked like an Old Master's drawing done in bitumen.

Sometime during that long night, Mother vowed, "If God lets me live through this, I'm takin' the children and goin' home." Father's silence indicated agreement. In spite of the magical world which appeared after the storm, in spite of the world of plenty, a contrast with the hard exacting life in the coal fields, the mountains seemed to offer safety and security.

The day after the blizzard dawned calm and sunny, the shadow of the barn across the road lay on the snow in vivid pink. The sun sprinkled fiery diamonds on the snow that covered the world. Father had gone down the hill to Aunt Betty's, and the school bus had picked up the children. I decided to make gingerbread and, finding there was no sugar, I thought I'd walk to get it at the village store about two miles away. The sunshine was warming the day when I set out in a fairy world.

The store was a large brick building with huge plate-glass windows. A tall, thin, white-haired man, Mr. Withey, worked there with two women clerks. Mr. Withey, who had courtly manners, noticed my hesitant entrance at the front door and came over to me when I leaned on the radiator to warm up.

We talked about the weather; Mr. Withey asked me if I lived in town. When I told him where I had come from, he seemed amazed that I had walked all that way. After I felt warmer, I asked him for five pounds of sugar. Mr. Withey went behind the counter and got it off the shelves. But instead of giving it to me, he carried the sugar with him to where a small office fitted into a corner in the back of the store.

When he returned, he was accompanied by a tall handsome man who seemd to be in his early forties. Mr. Withey introduced him as Howard Warren, the store's owner. "I've told him to drive you home," he said authoritatively. Mr. Withey, who was seventy-five years old, had worked for Howard's father for over thirty years.

I protested that I could walk home.

"Get your coat and boots on, Howard," Mr. Withey said. He took care of giving me the sugar, and walked me to the front door to wait for Mr. Warren's black Ford coupe.

On the way home, we drove through the narrow corridor of ice and snow and talked about the weather. The car suddenly skidded and slid sideways in the road, scaring me half to death. He laughed and patted my hand. Then he asked if I was married.

Our driveway hadn't been shoveled because we didn't have a shovel, but the children's feet had trampled down a path going to the bus. Howard Warren walked with me to the house and I introduced him to Mother. She offered him a chair near the big wood stove and thanked him for bringing me home. "I got worried when she got outta sight in all this ice." He didn't stay but a few minutes. He said later that the house had been too warm.

I answered a knock on the front door next morning about 11:30 and there stood Howard. He stepped in and stood on the doormat with his wet boots. "I came to ask if you'd go to lunch with me," he said, smiling.

"Well . . . er . . ." As I hesitated, he looked disappointed. I explained, "I have to ask Mother if I can go, she's in the kitchen." Mother returned with me and he asked her himself and she said yes. So we went to lunch.

The next day at 11:30 I answered the door and there he was again, asking me to go to lunch. Mother was sitting by the stove and with my back toward him I made a face at her to say yes and she did. After lunch we went to a bowling alley where he tried to teach me to bowl and then we went back for a late dessert at the restaurant. When I got home it was beginning to look like dark was coming, and Mother thought I'd been gone too long.

Howard had worked on Wall Street as a CPA for years, but was in California when his father died very suddenly, about two years before we met. His mother had died a few years before that of a kidney infection. His father willed him the store that had been designed and built by one of New York State's most prominent architects, Claude Bragdon of Rochester. When Howard returned from California, he moved into one of the two five-room apartments above the store.

In his little office in the back of the store, he kept track of his businesses: a house and a car repair shop at a railroad siding at the edge of the village, where he had also a large warehouse left to him by his grandfather, Simeon Howard; farmers rented the space to store apples and potatoes. It sat on a railroad siding at the edge of the village, where he also owned a house and car repair shop. In his little office at the store he kept track of these businesses.

Aunt Betty sent word to me one day that an elderly woman in the village was looking for live-in help. She had a housekeeper, but wanted someone who could read to her, write letters and do other personal things. "It don't pay much," my cousin said, "but it's a job." He drove me to Mrs. Hubbard's house in his truck to apply. She hired me and I started work the next day.

Mrs. Hubbard was the widow of a doctor who had willed everything they had to a Dr. Crawford to take care

of her for the rest of her life. On a little shelf across from
her bed stood a jasper jar with her husband's ashes in it.
The middle-aged housekeeper, Amelia, was a Czech who
spoke little English. She kept the house very clean. I sat
by the bed and read paperback novels to Mrs. Hubbard or
wrote as she dictated long rambling letters to her friends
in Lilydale who were mediums.

In early April my family went back to Kentucky. But
without me. I lacked a month being eighteen when in May,
Howard and I were married in the Victorian parlor of the
Presbyterian manse, witnessed by two of his friends.

I moved into his five-room apartment that had a hall-
way that seemed a mile long. I found myself cast into a
world I couldn't believe. My closet was overflowing with
clothes. The dressing table was covered with cosmetics:
perfumes, powder, lipsticks in various shades of pink, and
every other beauty aid a Yankee woman needed. When-
ever my conscience was pricked by the faraway voice of
Gideon telling me, "Lay not your treasures up on earth . . . ,"
I simply closed my ears and wrote another check.

I had sets of matching dishes, rugs underfoot, draper-
ies at the windows, and knickknacks covering every surface. We simply went to Rochester and bought what we
thought we needed. It was my husband who thought we
needed two sets of dishes, one for everyday, and one for
company.

Then he asked me to pick out a set of dessert dishes
for "evening company." After that, we had to buy a china
cabinet to put all these dishes in. I knew nothing about
buying anything, having had no experience of that in my
previous life in Kentucky, so I had to rely on what the

store clerks told me. My husband called this buying frenzy "setting up housekeeping."

Driving home one day from Rochester, the back seat heaped with purchases, my husband suddenly remarked, "I don't like mountains, and I don't like three-room shacks, but wouldn't you like to go to Kentucky for a visit? You could go on the train without me."

"I never want to set foot in Kentucky again," I declared with conviction. "The mud, the bare floors, the smoky old cookstoves. Why on earth would I ever want to go there again?"

He reached over and patted my knee. "Well, when you do . . ."

I assured him that I'd never go back there.

During the months following our wedding, my husband's friends invited us to one dinner party after another. I loved getting dressed up and going to these affairs. It was the first time in my life that I spent time in front of a looking glass, perhaps because it was the first time in my life that I had a choice about what to wear. No matter what I wore, however, I put on the little gold wristwatch my husband had given me. Its burnished glow and soft, almost inaudible ticking kept telling me "the time has changed." We went somewhere with friends almost every night of the week, and I learned to dance.

My husband mentioned all the dinners given for us and commented that he thought we should reciprocate.

"Reciprocate?" When he explained the word to me, I bought a big *Better Homes & Gardens Cookbook*, not only with recipes, but with a section of colored pictures and diagrams showing how to set dinner, lunch, and breakfast tables properly. I studied this book diligently and then cooked everything in it that appealed to us.

We were having six or eight people to dinner at a time. My husband chose the menu, and I marked the pages the recipes were on. He wrote a time schedule for me to follow: "First thing in the morning, get the Parker House rolls to rising; then make the lemon chiffon pie and set the table. In mid-afternoon, put the roast in the oven on low temperature; later, get dressed and cook the vegetables, lastly, make the salad." I memorized his instruction and, according to him, grew to be as expert at giving dinner parties as his mother had been.

Yes, this was the real world that I'd stepped into. The way it was meant to be and the way it was. The feeble stars of my childhood were outshone by the bright lights; the sound of the wind and flowing of Crase's Branch couldn't be heard over the Boogie Woogie music with its warm, insistent beat, and the pure, cold well water, or even Cindy's blackberry juice, was no match for scotch and soda in beautiful Waterford crystal.

Fate had set me in the middle of a throng of happy people who lived in a glorious new world—the "real" world—or so I thought.

It crept up on me so slowly and so insidiously that I couldn't put my finger on where the feeling was coming from. Was it my mind? My heart? Or was it seeping from my very soul? The only word that described it was "Aloneness." I'd begun to feel isolated and friendless in the very midst of all this frenzied entertainment, fun, and money. I became unresponsive, feeling as though I were viewing it all from a distance.

My possessions heaped up around me were now cold, dead ashes—the life burned out of them. And life had burned out of me, too. I picked at my food and made no more friendly overtures toward these "strangers" surrounding me. The bedrock I stood on had shifted precariously, leaving me tottering between two worlds: one was filled with beautiful things and security, while the other consisted of nothing more than a three-room shack filled with children and parents. I wanted to go home.

My husband noticed a change of attitude in me, and when he mentioned it, I brushed it off, thinking it was disloyal of me to turn against his way of life, especially since I had accepted it so willingly. And hadn't I told him, "I never want to set foot in Kentucky again"? Then, too, my diary referred to him as the Prince who married the milkmaid from Cindy's lane.

Homesickness had incapacitated me.

And then the letter came. It was written on splintery-textured rough paper with broad printed lines. I knew it had been written with a penny pencil sharpened with my father's pocket knife. I also knew that the eraser, when the pencil was worn to a stub, would be brand new, for spelling was nothing to worry about at home. Father had obviously written it with Mother sitting at the table, since I could tell her sentences from his. The interwoven sentences told me how much I was missed and that my parents would like me to come home for a visit. The letter was a lighted match to my volatile, repressed yearning to go home, and I burst into anguished tears.

When my husband came home from work, he found no dinner in the oven. Instead, I was in bed with red, swollen eyes, Father's letter under my pillow, and with a determination never to get up again.

He sat on the edge of the bed and looked at me in alarm. "What's wrong?"

"I want to go home." It came out defiant and angry.

He looked even more alarmed. "You mean you're leaving?"

"I want to see my mother and father," I responded, feeling like a ten-year-old.

He lifted my hand, kissed it, and, pulling a handkerchief from his pocket, wiped away the tears. Still holding my hand, he pulled me out of bed. "I'll call Batavia and get the train tickets while you pack and get ready to leave tomorrow. Now straighten yourself up and let's go out and get some dinner."

The statement was like a flood of water rinsing away the leaden feeling that had held me so long in its grip. As we sat in a Batavia restaurant, my eighteen-year-old confidence reasserted itself. No, I mustn't let an emotional encounter wipe out "common sense." I was going home, yes, but I couldn't just casually walk through the door. I had to make an impression, something to say "New York" and definitely not "Letcher."

"I can't go tomorrow or the next day," I told him. "I have to get a new dress and get my hair done."

The next day he sat in an armchair by the long mirror in the Better Dress department of Rochester's leading department store. He waited for me to come out of the dressing room, where the saleslady, in her black crepe dress and single strand of pearls, had taken me.

"I want something for summer travel," I had told her grandly. "In linen or cotton, and it has to be green."

Of the four garments she presented for approval, I chose two to try on. The first was a muted green linen suit with wide-cuffed short sleeves to the elbows. She fetched long beige gloves that met the sleeves of the jacket. "Accessories can make the dress," she said, returning with a wide-brimmed straw hat, also in beige, and with a green band that matched the color of the suit.

The narrow mirror told me that I looked older and very worldly, with not a vestige of girlishness remaining. Gee Whiz! I loved it! Nothing like this had ever been in the Montgomery Ward catalogs I had pored over in Miss Rainey's rocking chair. With her hand under my elbow, the saleslady guided me to the larger room where my husband sat. I stopped in front of the big mirror, hardly believing that the woman's reflection I saw was actually me. "What do you think?" I asked him.

"I think it's very, very beautiful."

After turning this way and that, studying the outfit from all angles in the mirror, I reluctantly went to try on the second choice. It was an imported Egyptian-cotton batiste in the palest of greens, having tiny green sprigs of darker green and a wide shawl collar of white organdy. The saleslady assured me that it was "the perfect dress for dinner on the terrace."

Thinking of Letcher, I confided, "I won't be going to any dinners on the terrace."

For the second time she led me to the other room with the bigger mirror. This dress gave me a whole new feeling and a whole new look. I felt light and flouncy and certainly looked younger than my eighteen years.

"It's very beautiful," my husband repeated.

It truly was, and I did look like an honest-to-God southern belle, but I had half my mind on the green linen suit that had New York sewn in every stitch and made me look so sophisticated and mature. With her index finger entwined in her pearls, the saleslady stepped closer. "It has a touch of femininity that is irresistible "

"Well, I . . ." biting my lower lip, I tried to make a momentous decision.

"We'll take them both," my husband told her.

I wouldn't have thought of that solution in a hundred years. On the way back to the dressing room, as through a misty veil, I vaguely heard Gideon, "Pride and vanity . . ."

"Clothes aren't really important," I defended myself to the saleslady.

"Clothes are everything."

Since my parents had no telephone, I had written a letter telling them I was coming home. But I couldn't tell them what day I'd be there because I was planning a grand arrival that was taking much time. When I got on a powerful new train, the Super Chief, in Buffalo, I found it cool and spotlessly clean. The dining car was shiny white with linen, crystal, and silver. For twenty five cents I could rent a huge, snowy goose-down pillow. The ladies lounge took up half a car and had a full-length mirror, which I used a dozen times to look at myself in the new outfit. Each time, the reflection assured me that I looked exactly the way a New York woman should look.

At Cincinnati I changed to a lesser train and crossed the Ohio River into Kentucky. The next morning, after we arrived in Winchester, I changed to an L&N train that travelled to the head of the Kentucky River. This was the train that I'd been waiting to get on: three coaches and a mail car pulled by a coal-burning engine. Only now was I really going home.

A warm feeling swept over me as I watched the people get on the train: the faded, loose cotton dresses of the women with their hair pulled up off their necks in knots; the gallused overalls the men wore, the buttons concealing an intense blue color where the sun couldn't reach. If Grant Wood had ever painted a group of Eastern Kentuckians going on a pilgrimage, this would have been the scene. As they found their seats, their voices mingled in soft inflections and nuances that I hadn't heard in so long that the train seemed filled with music.

I waited expectantly for one of them to sit beside me, preferably a mother with a baby for me to hold. However, they paused at my seat, glanced at me and walked on. When the train started moving, I sat alone in rejection. But I instinctively knew what they all thought—that I was the mine superintendent's wife.

The coal smoke from the engine blew back through the open windows, carrying black, gritty particles. This was one of my memories, and I breathed it all in. I couldn't take my eyes off the little three- and four-room houses that clung precariously, inside their fenced yards, to the sides of the mountains. Their little gates were fastened with loops of wire over the gateposts.

The conductor came down the aisle of the train. "You wantin' lunch, Ma'am?" There would be no stop for passengers at the next depot, but a dollar lunch would be put on the train. No, he didn't know what it would be, since it was different every day. After a jolting stop and jerking start, he handed me a white container, about the size of a shoebox, and a bottle of NeHi orange pop. The box contained fried chicken, candied sweet potatoes, coleslaw, and hot biscuits. The tin fork and napkin it was wrapped in both had L&N stamped on them and were to be collected later.

At four o'clock in the afternoon, I got off the train at Blackey, about two miles from home. No one met it, since I had left New York State sooner than expected. I stood in the shade of the depot's overhang till the train moved past me on its way to Whitesburg, then crossed its track and an adjacent spur that went only to Corbin Glow. I walked onto the weed-lined cinder path and followed the track to a two-story tower where trains stopped to take on water. There the tracks diverged just before reaching a long railroad trestle that crossed the Kentucky River, and there I returned to the track to cross the bridge. I approached it with anticipation since I'd crossed it a hundred times in the past, often pausing to look far down between the ties where the water flowed from around a mountain curve in a grinding, mumbling complaint.

Eagerly I stepped on the wooden ties but had gone only a few steps when I stopped and stood tottering precariously on a narrow tie in my "spike heel" shoes. I felt trapped till I recalled that I had always crossed before in bare feet to insure safe footing. Gingerly, I turned myself around on the narrow wooden tie and made my way back to solid ground where I could remove the "fashionable" New York shoes that were simply an impediment here.

Carrying the shoes and my purse in one hand and the heavy traveling bag in the other, I confidently started across again in my stocking feet. Feeling a slight breeze rustling my hair and tugging at my "cartwheel" hat, and having no free hand to hold it, I visualized my beautiful hat floating down the river. Retracing my steps a second time, I put the shoes, gloves and hat under a low bush where I knew they would be safe till I took the bag across and came back for them.

On the third attempt, I walked quickly to the middle of the bridge. From there, if I heard a train blowing a mile away, I could get off safely. My heart, as always, beat rapidly until I reached the halfway mark on the trestle. Then I relaxed and dawdled along, stopping a time or two to stare down at the brown and muddy river. It had rained somewhere, and the river, carrying a full load of silt, flowed with a thick, muffled sound. Like the color of the mountains, the sound of the river was everchanging.

Without the heavy bag, I skimmed back across the bridge and returned with my belongings. Sitting down on the end of a railroad tie and folding back the bottom of my linen skirt, I wiped my face on the hem of my silk slip. There were two lace-trimmed handkerchiefs still in their thin store boxes in my purse, each with a "W" embroidered in tiny white roses. I'd brought them for a special occasion. Perhaps at some point in the church service I would dab daintily at my forehead with a lacy square to show that I no longer wiped the sweat of my brow on a piece of old worn-out pillow slip. As I sat there I pondered how, for the first time in over a year, I was hot and sweaty, tired and thirsty, and yet as a monk might feel in his narrow cold cell, I was thankful. For this was the real feeling of this rough mountainous region: weariness tinged with sorrow, and it brought a deep sense of being home in Letcher. I accepted this feeling as willingly as I'd borne the wire bails cutting into my palms while I was carrying the milk pail from Cindy's lane. There was no easy way here. The easy way was far off in New York.

Blackey was out of sight behind me and Letcher was out of sight beyond the curve ahead. I sat alone on the weatherbeaten tie, feeling the heat of the hot steel rail at my back as I listened to the river's broken rhythm washing against the underpinnings of the high trestle.

I'm almost home, I thought, leaning my head back and lifting my eyes to the top of the mountain looming over me, its face already darkened with the shadow of the mountain behind me. I could feel a strange power hovering over these dark cliff-strewn mountains, a power that was as indomitable as nature herself. My New York finery lay strewn at my feet. The gloves lay across a steel rail, the hat was on a wooden tie, and the high heel shoes were thrown on the cinder path. My new hair-do hung damp and stringy. The people on the train had rejected me because of my clothes, and now the mountain railroad had stripped me of those pretentious garments.

Well, hadn't these mountains engendered me? Hadn't I overcome the cornfield? I combed my hair and put on the shoes, hat and gloves. Then, picking up the heavy bag, I started walking home on the little path beside the track. I hadn't gone but a short way when I saw Lydia Combs standing in knee-high grass across the creek. She was in her back yard, stirring apple butter on an enameled blue-and-white kitchen stove. I could smell it from where I was standing, remembering that Lydia always chose early apples, insisting "They's the best uns fer apple butter." A stove pipe about a yard high was attached to the stove to keep the smoke out of her face.

I crossed the wobbly, home-made bridge over Rockhouse Creek and, dropping my bag in the weeds, went through the tall grass toward her, my spike heels sinking an inch or two in the earth at every step, the weeds catching and clawing at my nylon stockings. Spying me, Lydia came with arms wide open to hug me. "I knowed you 'as a comin'. Yore daddy told me at the post office."

I followed as she hurried back to the stove and started stirring the apple butter vigorously. A large kettle of quart jars sat steaming at the side. I asked about her family, especially her three sons, Ivan, Raymond, and Lovell. "Ivan got married. Here, stir this a minute, honey, till I run in the house. I've got a likeness of the weddin'." She put the long wooden handle of the paddle in my gloved hand and sped across the yard.

The apple butter was nearly done. Thickened and beginning to stick to the bottom of the pan, it splashed and splattered till only constant stirring would calm it. A kitchen towel lay over a bramble bush near the stove, so I stuck it in the front of my skirt as an apron.

Lydia soon came flying back across the yard on legs as brown as a dried tobacco leaf and handed me the "likeness." Ivan was standing beside a beautiful woman, the two of them framed in gilt, and when I'd stared at it long enough to please her, Lydia took it and leaned it against the trunk of an old apple tree. With the apple butter ready to can and Lydia's full attention needed, I hung the towel on the bush and held out my hand. "You come back now," she said, squeezing my hand.

"I will, you come."

I walked back through the weeds, picked up my bag, and crossed the rickety bridge to the dusty road. When I crossed the railroad and took a narrow dirt road up and around the mountain that would bring me to our gate, the shade was already beginning to settle. I knew that at this hour Mother and the children would be on the front porch, but because of the tree-lined curve in the road they didn't see me till I was almost in front of the gate. Then they all came running down the steps and across the yard. I dropped my bag and, running to meet them, hugged and kissed everybody. Mother was teary-eyed as she kissed me. I picked up the baby and carried him to the swing on the porch, but he hadn't seen me in so long he'd forgotten me and wriggled down from my lap.

Mother sat down beside me. "You come by yourself?"

"We both couldn't leave at the same time. This way I can stay longer."

She sent one of the children to get me a fresh drink of water. Then, putting an arm around my shoulder, she said, "I'll get us a good supper tonight. When you rest a minute, I'll show you our garden. We've already got new taters and a lot of pole beans to cook with them."

I stood up and stretched out my gloved arms. "Mother, can't you see I'm not from here any longer? I'm from another place now . . . New York!"

"It won't ever matter where you are, Milady, you'll always be from here."

I knew when Mother called me "Milady" that I'd stepped out of line. I went into the house to put on a cotton skirt, a blouse, and a pair of sandals, then followed

Mother to the back yard where she put a hoe in my hand. It was the same hoe I had used so rebelliously in the mountain cornfield years earlier. I marveled at its smooth handle, pondering the distant hours; it had been a companion, adversary, or friend, to so many of our family. While I considered this and how foreign it seemed to my life as a New Yorker, Mother took an old basket off a nail on the back wall of the house and led me to the potato patch. I carefully dug into the hills of potatoes as she leaned over me holding the basket for me to put them in.

"Hit does a bidy good to come home, don't it?" Mother said, patting my shoulder.

I'd missed her, too.

About a week after I got back home, a letter came from Father telling us that my oldest brother James had bought a house in Castile, New York, about twenty miles from Wyoming, for them to live in and that they'd be coming there to live in Castile.

A while later they turned in that house for a down payment on a small farm in Pike near Castile. In both of these villages, the people befriended the Bailey family and helped in every way they could until one day, they stepped into mainstream America and got good jobs.

EPILOGUE

My father was a coal miner and at the age of sixty my father died of black lung. An unremembered office sent Mother a check for $3,000.

In July, 1992, I had a longing to see "the prettiest place on earth," Letcher, Kentucky, once more. I wanted, again, to stand at the foot of beautiful green mountains and stare upward. Leaving New York I arrived in Louisville and the next morning at seven, I started the journey on flat ground with miles and miles of huge tobacco plants alongside the road. (Ashtrays were on every table in every restaurant.) The speed limit was sixty-five m.p.h. instead of fifty-five: gasoline was 99¢ instead of $1.37 per gallon. As in Louisville, industries clustered around every town and city. The sun was warm and the people smiled at every stop.

I kept my eyes glued to the horizon for a glimpse of the mountains and after a two-hour drive to Campton, I suddenly saw a faint blue hint, so far in the distance there were no lines

Getting closer the blue hint turned to low foothills. On Kentucky's new four-lane Mountain Parkway, I went to Jackson, in Breathitt County. Father was born and raised there. The entrance to the town was planted with hundreds of flowers in full bloom. It was a beautiful welcome. As it wound in and out of the mountains, the Kentucky River lapped at the edge of Jackson. The streets were so straight up the hill that I shuddered to think what would happen in a two- or three-foot snowfall.

I had a friend from Letcher who now lived up the river from Jackson, in Vicco. For years, he and his wife had run a general store there. Vicco was an attractive village with many homes, a large church, a garage and a gas station. It sat on the very banks of the Kentucky River with only the railroad between. On the mountain was a narrow secondary road that lay between the village and the Mountain Parkway.

The bases of the mountains had been dynamited and bulldozed to level space for the big four-lane highway. Some of the cliffs left from this operation seemed half a mile high.

We hugged each other as only long-lost friends can, and then sat down for a long talk. I told him how easy it was to get here on the new road. His face fell. "I lost about eighty customers to that road. All of them lived on the other side and would have to drive miles and miles to get off it to get back to the store. They don't come anymore."

After getting information on motels in Whitesburg, I resumed my journey.

Leaving Vicco, I found an appalling and shocking scene on the road. The mountains had been hollowed out by the removal of millions of tons of coal, and now their outsides were being strip mined. Some of their peaks were being bulldozed down into saddle shapes, others were lop-sided because one side had been peeled off, leaving the appearance of half a mountain.

There were huge areas of raw, bare, yellow scars and the sun, like a light in a hospital operating room, focused on the cuts, scabs and bruises.

The land of Ohio, Indiana and parts of Kentucky was a level plain from which these beautiful mountains sud-denly rose majestically skyward. Their contribution to the uniqueness of the state of Kentucky was similar to the contribution of the Alps to the uniqueness of Switzerland. Now, many of them lay desolate in heaps of rubble. Dear God, night had truly come to the Cumberland. Kentucky, wrested from the Indians in such fierce battles that it had been called "Dark and Bloody Ground," had now, in this area, lost something that could never be replaced, and lost it without a skirmish.

Before reaching Whitesburg on the Mountain Park-way road at Isom, I turned onto the secondary road that followed Rockhouse Creek to Letcher, from where it went on to Blackey and emptied into the North Fork of the Kentucky River. I had traveled this road many times when we had called Rockhouse Creek "The River." But now driving on it seemed like driving on a road through the woods. Trees had grown up so thick along the roadway that in places they met in a green roof over the road, mak-ing it dark and gloomy.

The once deep, wide, clear "River" could be seen only intermittently through the wall of trees. They say that "see-ing is believing." I saw, but I couldn't believe. Silt had filled the river so full that tiny islands appeared throughout with shrubs and willows growing on them. The water from erosion had a murky color, and its movement was sluggish.

I said to myself, "I must be lost, this can't be the right road because that is not the river that I wrote about." That river was clear and deep and flowed with a powerful movement behind it. So much power indeed that I had once written that I could hear the boulders grinding on its bottom as I walked beside its bank, which was gleaming with sprays of wildflowers.

Driving on through that gloomy road I finally came to Letcher, to that place that Father had called "the prettiest place on earth."

As I entered Letcher I wasn't aware that I had passed Stuart Robinson School. It sat higher than the road that had been cut out of the hill, and the six-foot chain link fence that circled the campus was so heavily covered with vines that it looked like a solid green wail.

I turned left onto a narrow road that followed Crase's Branch up the holler toward the house of the only person left in Letcher that I knew. I stepped out of the car at his gate into a surrealist world that totally disoriented me. It was like stepping into the "Twilight Zone." The mountainsides, every tree and bush, every outbuilding and all the fences, were covered in kudzu vines. The woodlands under the trees had a three-foot layer of these vines. Their heavy green color seemed reflected in the very sky.

Uneasily, I asked my friend how these people put up with the vines. He said, "Nobody hunts anymore, and nobody goes in the woods anymore because of the snakes on the mountain floor under these vines." I didn't see any birds or squirrels anywhere.

Kudzu had been brought to the United States from Japan to be used for cow fodder in Georgia. It was touted for its nutrients and easy growth. It had spread wildly out of control. In Tennessee, Kentucky, Georgia and other states it has become a great nuisance.

Kudzu had helped to wipe out the best part of my childhood memories. The mountain behind our house where I struggled with the cornfield was totally covered in vines that had choked the trees in the field. The house at the foot of the hill which I had loved so much was no longer there. It had been wiped off the face of the earth by fire. The two little country stores were gone too. Crase's Branch was all but invisible through the jungle-like growth that muffled its tinkling, rocky music. The trees made no sound, the wind could no longer blow through their branches. There was an eerie stillness in mid-afternoon.

However, the houses that could be seen were neatly painted, with flowers in the yards and new, or good, cars parked in the front. Most of these people now worked in Whitesburg or Hazard because all the mines in this place had closed down. Indeed, the standard of living seemed higher that it had been when I had lived there.

When my friend met me at his gate, one of the first things I asked, was, "What happened to your big white gate with the trellis full of the five sisters roses?"

He smiled, shaking his head. "They all got old."

I asked him if he'd take me to the graveyard. "Hey, you wantin' to be buried here?" He laughed. The sun had lowered behind the peaks of the mountains throwing the eastern sides into shadows, as we walked to the cemetery. It was surrounded by blackberry and elderberry bushes and parts of a low wire fence. One outstanding tree, with the biggest trunk I'd ever seen, stood among the young saplings that had grown up in the graveyard. Some of its limbs, and quite a few of its branches, were missing.

Many of the tombstones were still, in August, covered with plastic flowers from Decoration Day. The first epitaph I read was Gideon's and the feeling I had of being so close to him again was overwhelming. He wasn't gone, he was still here and there beside him lay his wife, the beautiful and gentle Louizy. Wandering from stone to stone, I found many of the people I'd spent two years writing about. We were, in a way, "reunited in death."

Only two of my schoolmates were here. They had both died of polio. The others, like me, had long ago left Letcher.

Thanking my friend and bidding him goodbye, I went down the road to Blackey, where I stopped at a general store that sold groceries, gas and cowfeed. I bought a cola that I took to the big front porch and sat in a rocking chair drinking it. The owner, Mr. Caudill, came out and sat in the swing near me. His family had owned this store for over a hundred years. It perched at the foot of a hill on a narrow road that ran alongside the Kentucky River, with Blackey on the other side. We talked on and off until he left to wait on another customer and I went on my way.

The morning sun rising from the top of the mountain softly fused the misty valleys to the hills and put a glister on Cindy's dew-sprinkled roof. The shiny trodden paths on her hillside had all disappeared into paw-paw and elderberry bushes. The houses beside her road were empty now, and covered with green vines of the creeping kudzu.

Sitting on the porch in the early morning sun, her hair snow white and with a walking stick hung over the arm of her rocking chair, she stared into the green void. Her dim eyes searched out my voice and then she found my face. We remembered what it had been, and dear God, we wondered where it had all gone.